Unl

Assessment

The Unlocking Series
Series Editor: Robert Fisher

Robert Fisher was until recently Professor of Education and Director of the Centre for Research in Teaching Thinking at Brunel University. His research publications on teaching and thinking are internationally recognised and he has published more than twenty books on education. His recent publications include *Teaching Thinking* (Continuum) and the highly acclaimed *Stories for Thinking* series (Nash Pollack). He is involved in research and training with schools and local education authorities, is an adviser to the Department for Education and Skills and is a frequent speaker at national and international conferences on the teaching of literacy, creativity and thinking skills.

Also available:

Unlocking Creativity
Teaching across the curriculum
Edited by Robert Fisher and Mary Williams
1-84312-092-5

Unlocking Learning and Teaching with ICT
Identifying and overcoming barriers
Helena Gillespie
1-84312-376-2

Unlocking Speaking and Listening
Edited by Pamela Hodson and Deborah Jones
1-84312-392-4

Unlocking Writing
A guide for teachers
Mary Williams
1-85346-850-9

Unlocking
Assessment

Understanding for reflection and application

Edited by Sue Swaffield

Routledge
Taylor & Francis Group

LONDON AND NEW YORK

First published 2008
by Routledge
2 Park Square, Milton Park, Abingdon, Oxon OX14 4RN

Simultaneously published in the USA and Canada
by Routledge
270 Madison Ave, New York, NY 10016

Routledge is an imprint of the Taylor & Francis Group, an informa business

Typeset in Bembo by Wearset Ltd, Boldon, Tyne and Wear
Printed and bound in Great Britain by T.J. International Ltd, Padstow, Cornwall

British Library Cataloguing in Publication Data
A catalogue record for this book is available from the British Library

Library of Congress Cataloging in Publication Data
Unlocking assessment: understanding for reflection and application/edited by Sue Swaffield.
p. cm.
1. Educational tests and measurements. I. Swaffield, Sue.
LB3051.U58 2008
371.26–dc22
2007034244

ISBN10: 0-415-45313-5 (pbk)
ISBN10: 0-203-93093-2 (ebk)

ISBN13: 978-0-415-45313-4 (pbk)
ISBN13: 978-0-203-93093-9 (ebk)

Contents

Contents

Illustrations

Figures

Tables

About the contributors

Margaret Carr is Professor of Education at the University of Waikato, New Zealand. She co-directed the New Zealand Te Whāriki early childhood curriculum project, and has worked with teachers in a number of research projects on learning and assessment in the early years.

Mary-Jane Drummond was an infant teacher for many years before she joined the Faculty of Education at the University of Cambridge, from which she has recently retired. She has taught on a wide variety of professional development courses, specialising in the early years of childhood.

Pete Dudley taught in East London and abroad for many years before working as a primary and assessment adviser in Essex and later Deputy Director of Education Redbridge, London. He worked on school networks with NCSL and is now Director of the Primary National Strategy. He is a TLRP researcher and writer on primary education.

Lorna Earl, PhD is Director of Aporia Consulting Ltd. She is a recently retired Associate Professor and Head of the International Centre for Educational Change at OISE, University of Toronto. Assessment has been her career passion and she has written many articles, books and monographs on this topic.

Wynne Harlen has been involved in research, curriculum development and assessment throughout her career. The posts she has held include Sidney Jones Professor and Head of the Education Department at the University of Liverpool and Director of the Scottish Council for Research in Education. She is now Visiting Professor at the University of Bristol.

Jeremy Hodgen taught mathematics in primary and secondary schools, before joining King's College London where he teaches on the PGCE, MA and doctoral programmes. His research interests include assessment, learning and teaching in mathematics education. He is co-author (with Dylan Wiliam) of *Mathematics Inside the Black Box* (2006).

Mary James is Chair of Education at the Institute of Education, London and Deputy Director of the ESRC Teaching and Learning Research Programme. She currently holds an ESRC Research Fellowship and she is a member of the Assessment Reform Group.

Steven Katz is Senior Lecturer in Human Development and Applied Psychology at OISE/UT where he is also the coordinator of the Psychology of Learning and Development initial teacher education programme component, and a director of Aporia Consulting Ltd. He has received the Governor General's medal for excellence in his field and is co-author of *Leading Schools in a Data-Rich World*.

Martin Ripley is Director of the Student Academy at the National Academy of Gifted and Talented Youth (NAGTY). He is also a Director of the eAssessment Association and co-founder of the 21st Century Learning Alliance.

Sue Swaffield is a lecturer in Leadership and School Improvement at the University of Cambridge Faculty of Education. Assessment development and research has been a major theme throughout her career as a teacher, local authority adviser and now in higher education.

Mary Webb is Senior Lecturer in Information Technology in Education at King's College London and Director of the secondary PGCE ICT course. Previously she has taught ICT and science in secondary schools and all subjects in primary schools. Her research interests include pedagogy with ICT and formative assessment. She is co-author of *ICT Inside the Black Box* (2007).

Dylan Wiliam is Deputy Director, and Professor of Educational Assessment, at the Institute of Education, University of London. In a varied career, he has taught in inner-city schools, trained teachers, developed national curriculum assessments and undertaken a range of administrative tasks in universities. His main current interest is how to support teachers in making greater use of assessment to support learning.

Acknowledgements

We thank the many thousands of young people, teachers and colleagues we have worked with over the years, who have helped shape our thinking and deepen our understanding.

Introduction

Sue Swaffield

Assessment has always been with us as an integral part of learning, teaching, schooling and education. In recent years it has become more pervasive and prominent, becoming a focus of attention for pupils, parents, practitioners, researchers, policy makers and the media.

Assessment is multifaceted and complex. It comes in a variety of guises, takes many forms and fulfils a number of purposes. A commonly drawn distinction is between summative and formative purposes – often referred to as assessment *of* learning and assessment *for* learning. Both are important and both feature in this book, although the emphasis is on assessment to support learning.

The purpose of this volume is to aid three processes – the understanding of assessment, reflection on the issues and application to practice. In so doing it may unlock accepted but limiting ways of thinking, unravel taken-for-granted practices, and open up new ideas and approaches. It is aimed predominantly at teachers, but with young people as the most important beneficiaries.

The book can of course be read from cover to cover, and there is a logic to its sequence, and many connections among the chapters. However, the chapters can be read in any order depending on interest and relevance at a particular time. It is hoped that this is a book that will be returned to over time, to revisit issues and to explore new ones. Each chapter starts with a question or statement that captures its 'big idea', and 'points for reflection' (either towards the end of the chapter or scattered throughout) also give an indication of the ground covered and issues discussed. Reflection can be undertaken alone, but dialogue around the suggested points is likely to be stimulating and fruitful. Points of interest can be followed up through the references, and lists and sources of 'further reading' provide particular suggestions.

The contributors all have a wealth of experience, and include leading international experts in assessment. They share a continuing quest to explore the issues and deepen understanding, but their voices are distinctive, adding to the richness of the book. There are tensions between some of the viewpoints, and a few unresolved dilemmas, as is to be expected with something as complex and dynamic as assessment. Where the context is made explicit it is for the most part England, but assessment and its issues cross national boundaries. Indeed, there is much to be learned from practice developed in other countries and the ways that educators elsewhere have responded to policy challenges.

The book is structured in three sections. Part I considers assessment and its relationships with values, learning and agency. Mary-Jane Drummond opens the first chapter with a powerful and arresting story about a six-year-old child. It paves the way for the central theme of the chapter, that assessment involves making choices about children, achievement and learning, as well as choices about assessment practice. Drummond argues that there is a close relationship between assessment and our values and principles, and that we should ensure our actions reflect our values. In Chapter 2, Mary James explores three models of learning, and clearly explains their implications for assessment. She emphasises the importance of assessment practice being consistent with our beliefs about learning, and aligned with the kinds of learning students undertake. 'Fitness for purpose' is vital. The messages from the first two chapters are carried through into Chapter 3, where Margaret Carr urges us to consider how learning and assessment support young people in facing complex situations and prepare them for an unknown future. In a rich chapter she provides many extracts from 'learning stories' – a narrative approach to assessment that has been developed in Carr's native New Zealand. These stories vividly record and analyse critical episodes of learning, and foster children's developing agency.

Part II focuses upon assessment for learning, where assessment is an integral part of everyday learning and teaching, and its prime purpose is to support learning. In Chapter 4 Sue Swaffield contends that feedback is the central process in assessment, and makes links with other chapters in the volume. She discusses the powerful influences that feedback has on learning and achievement, pointing out that its effects can be negative as well as positive. We therefore need to understand its complexities and strive for feedback that promotes rather than frustrates our educational aims. Oral feedback in the form of questioning and dialogue is the topic addressed in Chapter 5 by Jeremy Hodgen and Mary Webb. They draw on research that they and colleagues in the assessment group at King's College London have undertaken, in order to identify key points about questioning and dialogue. Lesson transcripts bring practice to life and illuminate the detail. In Chapter 6, Lorna Earl and Steven Katz make the case for self-monitoring and self-regulation being at the core of learning, and argue that teachers need to help learners become their own best assessors. They relate their ideas to current learning theory, point to how students can develop the skills of self-assessment and provide three examples for reflection and discussion. Interpreting and using assessment data are the twin themes of Chapter 7 by Pete Dudley and Sue

Swaffield. They begin by examining some issues key to understanding data, and look at the various ways in which schools are using information from assessment to support learning and teaching. Reference is made to the growing bank of resources available to assist the process, and the chapter concludes with a set of principles to guide practice.

Part III addresses three very important assessment issues, picking up points made in earlier chapters and going into greater depth. In Chapter 8 Dylan Wiliam asserts that the quality of decisions we make on the basis of assessment is dependent on the quality of the assessment, and then through accessible examples clearly explains a number of important concepts. He argues that validity is central to evaluating the quality of assessment, and that validity is not a property of assessment itself, but rather of the inferences we make on the basis of assessment. Chapter 9 by Wynne Harlen looks at the relationship between formative and summative assessment, reminding us that the differences are about purpose, not forms of assessment. She makes the case for using teachers' judgements for summative assessment, and explains how the same evidence can be interpreted in different ways to serve different purposes. Teachers discussing evidence relating to individual students is beneficial for moderating summative judgements, as well as improving the process of formative assessment. In the final chapter (10) Martin Ripley looks ahead to a future where technology helps transform learning and assessment, as well as pointing out the difference that it is already making. He provides illustrations of practice, lists a number of benefits, summarises research in the area and outlines the policy framework. Ripley argues that e-assessment has much to offer, cannot be ignored and should be incorporated into our plans for the future of learning.

These ten chapters provide an authoritative overview of assessment, an informed exploration of key issues and accessible guidance for practice. A book can do much to open up understanding and encourage reflection, but application requires practical action, which in turn opens the doors to further understanding and reflection. These ideas are the subject of the final piece in the volume, 'Continuing the exploration'.

PART I

Assessment, values, learning and agency

Assessment and values

A close and necessary relationship

Mary-Jane Drummond

There is a close and necessary relationship between what we choose to assess and what we value most in the education of our children.

In this chapter I explore a proposition made many years ago in a lecture given by Professor Marten Shipman to the Primary Education Study Group (Cullingford, 1997); he claimed that 'there is a close and necessary relationship between what we choose to assess and what we value most in the education of our children'. The exploration opens with a story about a six-year-old child whom I knew well; his story introduces the theme of choice that runs through the rest of the chapter. My argument is that in the effective practice of assessment, educators make principled and value-driven choices about children, about learning and achievements. As a result they are able to make well-judged choices about the methods, purposes and outcomes of assessment.

Tom's story

First, the story. Its hero is a boy called Tom who attended the school where I worked in the early 1980s, an infant school for four- to seven-year-olds, with all the trappings of the English school system, which almost alone in Europe brings very young children into institutions closely modelled on the secondary school: long corridors, cellular classrooms, sealed off with doors, daily whole school assemblies, attendance registers and a statutory National Curriculum. I was the headteacher of this school.

Tom was regarded by all the staff as a difficult child to teach, as indeed he was, due to two distinct allergic conditions from which he suffered a good deal: he was allergic to both instruction and authority. These afflictions meant that although he attended school regularly and took part in many of the activities on offer, it was always on his terms and conditions, and never as the result of a teacher's directive. Once we had recognized the severity of Tom's condition, we managed to find ways of co-existing, though not without frequent confrontations and highly visible incidents of various kinds. There was, in effect, a permanent power struggle taking place, around the quality of Tom's life as he wanted to live it, and the life we wanted him to lead inside our benevolent and, we believed, inviting and challenging school setting.

The story begins when Tom was six, an age when in most of Europe children are still in nursery or kindergarten, or just beginning primary school. In contrast Tom had already had two-and-a-half years of full-time schooling and was now in the final year of key stage 1, the first stage of primary education. He was due to leave us in a few months for the next stage: a junior school on a separate site with a highly formal and rigid approach. Unfortunately for his prospects at the new school, Tom was not yet reading and writing independently. Indeed he had barely ever been known to pick up a pencil, though he loved to spend time with books, but always alone, far from the teacher's pedagogic gaze.

One day I spent the morning working alongside the teacher in Tom's classroom, time that included a long conversation with Tom about the model he was making with Lego. It was a massive spaceship of military design, bristling with rockets and other offensive weapons. Our conversation turned to the problem of military might and the threat of nuclear destruction. I have yet to explain that although Tom had not yet mastered the alphabet, his use of spoken language was prodigious, and he was a truly interesting person with whom to discuss current events on the social and political scene.

Back to the classroom: we talked about the possibility of global disarmament. Tom's opinion was that the power of the arms trade made disarmament unlikely. And so we talked on, until Tom concluded the discussion with a fine summary: 'And that's why the world is a mess.' My reply was, I hope, encouraging: 'Why Tom, that would be a fine title for a book. You write it, I'll publish it, and we'll split the profits.' At which point I took my leave.

Some hours later, when I was at my office desk working on some papers, I noticed Tom at the doorway. I immediately assumed the worst, that he had committed some dreadful crime against the world of school and had been sent to a higher authority to be admonished. So I was not welcoming, and Tom, in his turn, was offended and indignant. He reminded me of our earlier conversation: 'I have come to write that book!' I changed my tune at once and supplied him with a clean exercise book. He sat down at a table across the room from my desk, I entered the title of the book on the contents page, and at this point was dismissed back to my own work. This is the completed contents page, which he wrote some weeks later.

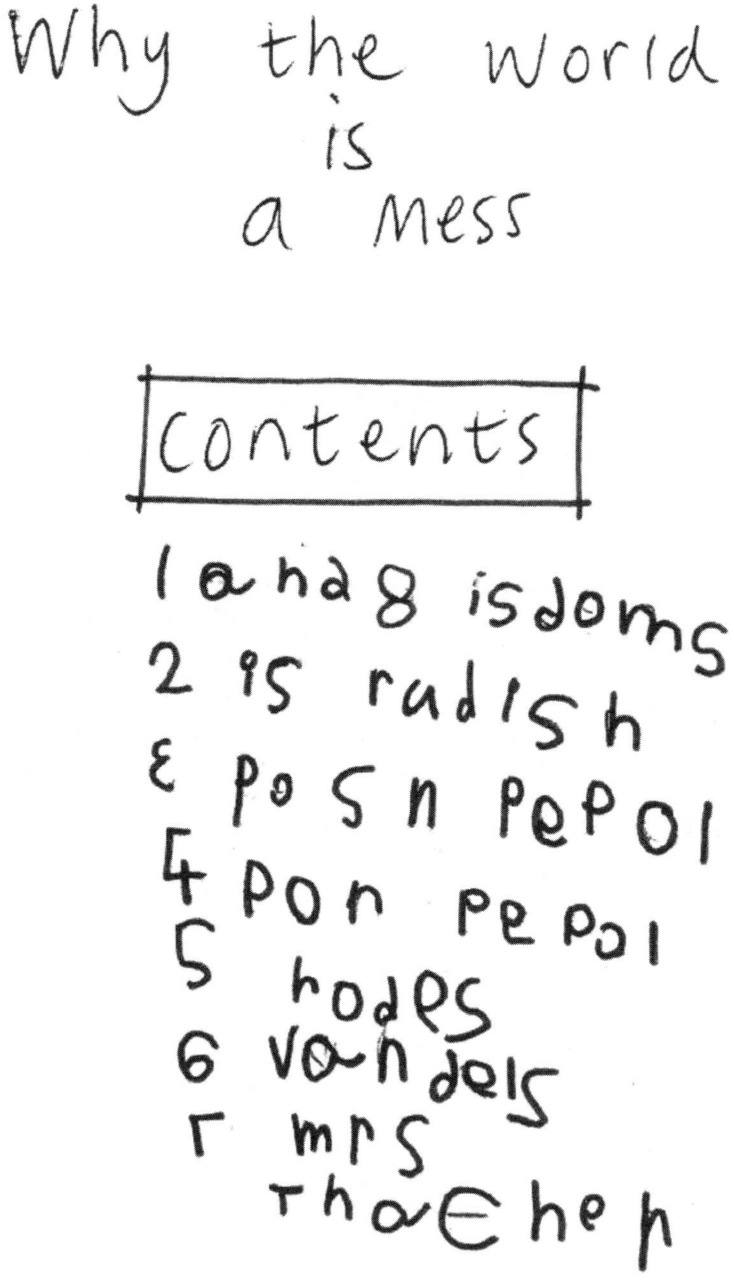

Why the world
is
a mess

Contents

1 a ha 8 isdoms
2 is radish
ε po s n pepol
4 pon pe pol
5 hodes
6 vandels
r mrs
Thae he h

FIGURE 1.1 The contents page of Tom's book.

[The text refers to the eight chapters of the book, thus:

1.   1 and 8 is bombs

2.   is rubbish

3.   posh people

4.   poor people

5   robbers

6   vandals

7   Mrs Thatcher.]

He needed a great deal of support in this production, never having written by himself before, to our knowledge. But word by word and letter by letter, Tom constructed this text. It took him many hours over several weeks: the extracts in Figure 1.2 give a flavour of his arguments.

At last the great work was complete, and Tom set off around the school to read his book to anyone who would listen. As his teachers should have predicted long before, Tom went on to flourish as both an accomplished writer and reader. It was the role of pupil he objected to, and with some reason.

Let me move on and draw out the moral of this story, with the hindsight of 20 years more experience and reflection. I now see Tom's story as a challenging illustration of some of the crucial choices that educators face in the practice of assessment:

● choices about children and their achievements
● choices about learning
● choices about the methods, purposes and outcomes of assessment.

Choices about children

First then, I argue that we have choices to make in the way in which we construct our understanding of what it is to be a child, what sort of people we think

From Chapter 1	Weapons are violent. It would be better if all governments said no to weapons.
From Chapter 3	There is not enough sharing.
From Chapter 9 (about racial issues, a later addition)	I think it is typical the way black people are treated. The black people get the worst houses and the worst jobs. On top of that, they get called names.

FIGURE 1.2 Extracts from Tom's book (spelling and punctuation corrected).

children are and what are their most salient qualities. Obviously the choices are limitless: we are assailed by possibilities. The Japanese set us an interesting example in their chosen word for the solution to this knotty problem: they speak of a 'child-like child' (*Kodomorashii Kodomo*). A full and fascinating account of this concept is given in an anthropological study: *Preschool in Three Cultures* (Tobin *et al.*, 1989), which critically explores beliefs about children held by educators in Japan, China and the USA. Other authors have more recently elaborated on this theme; for example, Dahlberg *et al.* (1999) offer a fascinating analysis of conflicting constructions of children and childhood, which includes a description of the child as an empty vessel, or *tabula rasa*, who is to be made 'ready to learn' and 'ready for school' by the age of compulsory schooling. In contrast to this child, whom the author call 'Locke's child', they position 'Rousseau's child', an innocent in the golden age of life. 'Piaget's child' is the scientific child of biological stages, while their preferred construction is of 'the child as co-constructor of knowledge, identity and culture'. Their argument is, like mine, that 'we have choices to make about who we think the child is and these choices have enormous significance since … they determine the institutions we provide for children and the pedagogical work that adults and children undertake in these institutions' (Dahlberg *et al.*, 1999: 43). Moss and Petrie (2002) revisit these categorizations of childhood, and argue that our current constructions of children's services are all based on the child who is 'poor, weak and needy'. As a result, these services 'are not provided as places for children to live their childhoods and to develop their culture' (Moss and Petrie, 2002: 63).

Baseline profile

LANGUAGE
1. Understanding words
    a) cannot understand simple words
    b) average understanding of words
    c) above average understanding

2. Following instructions
    a) inability to follow simple instructions
    b) able to follow familiar instructions
    c) able to follow involved instructions

3. Memory
    a) very poor memory, limited recall
    b) acceptable recall
    c) excellent, with immediate and delayed recall

FIGURE 1.3 Extract from a baseline profile schedule.

Another way of reading and understanding our working constructions of children and childhood is by scrutinizing the instruments we use to assess their learning. My own collection of assessment schedules designed to be used with young children on entry to school, amassed over many years, suggests that the English child-like child is required to be, amongst other things, fully responsive to verbal commands and instructions: in a word, obedient.

The instrument in Figure 1.3, for example, designed by a headteacher (Bensley and Kilby, 1992) to assess four-year-olds on entry to primary school, implies that language development can be assessed by observing the individual child's capacity to respond correctly to instructions, a highly contestable view. But this example is by no means unique, as we can see in Figures 1.4 and 1.5, where the capacity to obey is explicitly prioritized as being in need of assessment.

COMMUNICATION
LISTENING AND TALKING

1	2	3	4	5

1. Understanding
   instructions

Cannot follow instructions when addressed individually.	Can always follow a single instruction when addressed individually.	Can remember and follow instructions.

FIGURE 1.4 Extract from an early assessment instrument.

DATE OF PROFILE: .... DOB: ....

		1	2	3	4	5
Communication Listening and talking	1. Understanding instructions					
	2. Retention of oral information					
	3. Articulation					
	4. Understanding of words					
	5. Use of language: word order					
	6. Use of language: to convey meaning					

FIGURE 1.5 Extract from an early assessment instrument.

On any of these schedules, it is plain, Tom would be assessed as an entirely inadequate child, who is blatantly deviant from the expected norm. If Tom were to be assessed using the more recent Foundation Stage Profile (QCA, 2003) his strengths, for example in relation to personal, social and emotional development, would be more likely to be recognized, and his attempts at writing acknowledged.

There is another source of evidence for my claim that one prevailing concept of childhood is characterized by submissiveness and compliance: in a disturbing book, *Children into Pupils*, Mary Willes reports a classroom-based study, in which she followed children through their first months in school, documenting in great detail the process that transforms them from children to pupils. Her conclusion is stark: 'Finding out what the teacher wants, and doing it, constitute the primary duty of a pupil' (Willes, 1983: 138).

We may detect a note of exaggeration here, but only a note: the insight rings true. Willes' argument powerfully reinforces mine: that educators may choose to construct children as seriously inadequate until proved otherwise, until they show the signs of successful pupils – obedience, attentiveness, compliance and industry. On all of these counts, Tom would not score highly, if at all. But there is an alternative. We can, if we so choose, construct our images of children in a different mould. We can choose to see them as essentially divergent, rather than convergent, inner-directed, rather than other-directed, and competent, rather than incompetent.

In recent years, we have come to associate this construction with the work of the preschool educators in Reggio Emilia, Italy, though it is important to remember it has its roots in many earlier theorists, from Dewey to Piaget, and, significantly for us in England, the great Susan Isaacs (1930, 1933), whose hallmark was that she studied children as they really are, not as some of their teachers would like them to be. Here is an illustrative passage from Carlina Rinaldi, until recently Director of Services to Young Children in Reggio, which encapsulates the Reggio position on the most appropriate way to conceptualize the state of childhood: 'The cornerstone of our experience is the image of children as rich, strong and powerful ... They have the desire to grow, curiosity, the ability to be amazed and the desire to relate to other people' (quoted in Edwards *et al.*, 1993).

In a more recent book, Rinaldi (2006) elaborates this distinctive theme in the Reggio philosophy, while acknowledging the influence of both Vygotsky and Piaget, and, later, Bruner, Gardner and Hawkins. She argues that 'the image of the child' is, above all, 'a cultural and therefore social and political convention', which makes it possible for educators to give children the experiences and opportunities ('the space of childhood', 'a space of life') that give value to their qualities and their potential, rather than negating or constraining them. 'What we believe about children thus becomes a determining factor in defining the education contexts offered to them' (Rinaldi, 2006: 83). And part of those contexts, in our own schools and classrooms, is our practice of assessment.

Now if we return to Tom's story, and examine his learning through the lens of the Reggio 'image of the child', we see a very different picture. We see Tom as a child rich in knowledge and understanding, not just in terms of an extensive technical and expressive vocabulary and complex use of language, but in terms of his conceptual range and political understanding. His strength of will is remarkable, if inconvenient for his teachers; the strength of his resistance to authority cannot be denied, though we might (and certainly did at the time) wish it less strong. Tom's powers are no less remarkable: we may note, among others, those listed in Figure 1.7 below.

Choices about achievement

And Tom's achievements? There are choices to be made here too, in identifying and understanding what Tom can and cannot yet do. If we measure him against any kind of standard for effective literacy, we can easily identify his deficits. His writing is far from correct. There are letter reversals, many spelling errors, no capital letters or punctuation; by some standards, this is all very shocking. But the achievement remains. Tom's first written text is a coherent book, nine chapters long, fired with a sense of social justice and driven by his inner convictions, not by the directives of the curriculum, or the artificial audience of the teacher who needs Tom to write in order to provide material on which to assess him. There are no *standards* by which to measure Tom's achievement; it is unique, unpredictable, magnificent. It is worth remembering here that in 1933, the splendid Hadow Report on Infant and Nursery Schools, the sadly neglected forerunner of Plowden (CACE, 1967), took a very firm line on the undesirability of standards in the education of children of Tom's age: 'In none of this should a uniform

---

Tom's powers

- to persist and persevere
- to organize his thinking and his arguments
- to compare and contrast
- to recognize the big ideas in our complex society
- to strive for social justice
- to project his thoughts into the lives of others
- to care for his environment
- to reason and persuade

          . . . and more, much more.

FIGURE 1.6 Tom, a powerful child.

standard to be reached by all children be expected. The infant school has no business with uniform standards of attainment' (Board of Education, 1933: para. 105).

But in looking at children's achievements, whether or not we choose to measure them against any arbitrary level or standard, there is another consideration to be borne in mind. We need to decide how the judgements we make in assessing achievement are to be used. I have argued at length in the past (Drummond *et al.*, 1992; Drummond, 2003) that the best use we can make of our close observations and careful analysis of children's learning is, first, to help us understand what is going on, for individuals, groups and even whole classes of children, and, second, more crucially, to plough this understanding back into our provision, our curriculum, our pedagogy, our individual and group interactions.

Unfortunately, there are many other uses to which the instruments of assessment can also be put. Particularly dangerous, in my view, is the apparently built-in assumption that defining, labelling or measuring what a child can do today (or, more often, cannot do) is a completely reliable predictor of what she or he will do tomorrow – or at the moment of the next statutory assessment. If, however benevolent our intentions, we fall into a habit of thinking that the present dictates the future, that current achievement is commensurate with so-called ability, a fixed and unreachable entity within each child, that children's so-called levels of achievement at the age of four or five, or six or seven, tell us anything about what is to happen in the future, we are colluding in a deterministic and profoundly anti-educational enterprise. Our priorities should be to fight the predictions that the bean-counters make on our behalf, not to concur with them. 'Some children will never get a level 4', said a primary school headteacher to me, not long ago, as we discussed the school's involvement in the Learning How to Learn project (James *et al.*, 2007). Professional courtesy prevented me from replying as I would have wished:

> But it's the responsibility of the community of teachers in the school to work together to break down these limiting and damaging expectations. It's the responsibility of the staff group to enquire into what it is – in their curriculum, their pedagogy, their interactions, their assessment practices – that limits children's learning to this extent.

Luckily for Tom, whose breakthrough to literacy took place in 1984, long before the invention of SATs, league tables and the rest of today's assessment industry, his teachers were not under any pressure to predict his future as a learner in terms of levels of achievement, let alone his so-called ability. We were free to think and act for ourselves in our assessment practice, preferring to look at the big picture of his achievements in thinking, argument, communication, perseverance and care. We were confident that a child who was so powerful in these domains would, in due course, master the capital letter and the full stop. But today, when we do have statutory requirements to meet in our assessment practices, it seems to me that we have abandoned our capacity to think and act for ourselves in supplementing the narrow, arid, prescribed testing procedures with broader, more humane accounts of unpredictable and highly worthwhile learning – such as Tom's.

Choices about learning

I have used the story of Tom to illustrate the possibility of making choices in the ways in which we assess children and their achievements that are congruent with the 'Shipman principle', the close and necessary relationship between assessment and our core educational values. There are still more choices to consider. Underpinning our thinking about children is our understanding of the learning that they do. In trying to understand children's learning, we have a rich and wild variety of models and metaphors to choose from, some of which will serve children's interests better than others. In recent years, English educators in the Foundation Stage have been offered the constructs of 'early learning goals' and 'stepping stones' (QCA, 2000). Indeed, since 2006 these constructs have become embedded in the new requirements for the Early Years Foundation Stage, which come into force in 2008 (DfES, 2007). I have argued elsewhere (Drummond, 2003) that these approaches do less than justice to the significant qualities of children's learning: its unpredictability, its inventiveness and creativity, its purposefulness and emotional engagement.

Furthermore, my own observations in Foundation Stage classrooms, especially in Year R, the year in which children turn five (see for example, Adams *et al.*, 2004), suggest very strongly that for many educators, the achievement of individual learning goals, via the 'stepping stones', predetermined in the daily/weekly/monthly lesson plans, is a much higher priority than identifying or celebrating unforeseen, spontaneous, individual acts of making meaning. Children's growing understanding of the big ideas that really matter to them (so clearly illustrated in Tom's story) is not represented in the predefined ends embodied in the 'early learning goals'. These 'goals' are just not rich or complex enough to use as a way of understanding what powerful learners do when their 'education contexts' are good enough for them. For understanding 'rich, strong and powerful' learning, to use Rinaldi's phrase, we need to find other approaches, more promising possibilities.

Michael Armstrong's long-awaited book, *Children Writing Stories* (2006), offers just such a possibility. In this treasure-chest of children's writing, brilliantly analysed and interpreted, Armstrong aims to 'reach a fresh understanding of narrative understanding'. In his earlier work, *Closely Observed Children*, first published in 1980, Armstrong documented the intellectual life of a class of eight- and nine-year-old children in a rural primary school; he demonstrated how 'the seriousness of purpose' that he witnessed in the children's thinking and doing bore fruit in every aspect of their learning 'in their writing, their art, their mathematics, their model-making, their nature study' (Armstrong, 2006: ix). The new book narrows the focus: here Armstrong explores children's written narratives, and maps the 'creative and critical force of children's narrative imagination'. There are stories from children aged from five to 16, each examined respectfully, attentively, admiringly. Armstrong elucidates the passion and the purpose of each child's learning. In the concluding chapter he argues that 'Children's achievement as storytellers has radical consequences for an understanding of intellectual growth' (Armstrong, 2006: 174).

Armstrong uses the evidence he has laid before the reader to demolish the notion that education is best thought of as the initiation of passive, immature, irrational children into their society's culture. The children whose stories Armstrong has collected here are nothing of the kind; 'they are cultural participants … it is just because they have something to say that they are learning to say it so well'. He quotes Clifford Geertz to take his argument further: '[education] is not so much providing something the child lacks, as enabling something the child already has: the desire to make sense of self and others' (Armstrong, 2006: 174); he positions Geertz's term 'desire' in relation to his own work. The stories children tell show that 'narrative lies at the centre of children's response to this desire' (Armstrong, 2006: 174–5). This way of looking at learning, as an expression of desire, as a passionate search for meaning, with creativity at its centre, fundamental to the process, is a very long way indeed from the simplistic notion of 'learning goals' identified by adults, to be arrived at one by one, down the pathways of 'stepping stones'. Armstrong's way of looking at learning is imbued with his conviction of the powers of the learner; it is shot through with big ideas (companionship, beauty, ambiguity, authority); there is no question of quantifying these children's learning with any kind of scales or measures.

Another important alternative possibility is to be found in the work of writers and educators in New Zealand; their curriculum guidelines for early childhood, adopted in 1996, a bilingual document known as Te Whāriki, has stimulated great interest in other early years professional communities around the world. In a stimulating chapter in this volume one of the co-authors of these guidelines, Margaret Carr, describes her recent work on learning dispositions, particularly resourcefulness and agency. These challenging categories have emerged from developmental work with many educators over many years: here it is appropriate to go back to the source of Carr's current insights and difficult questions, and the approach to learning described in her important book *Assessment in Early Childhood Settings* (Carr, 2001). It was here that she introduced English readers to an approach to early learning based on narrative, in which the dominant metaphor is

---

Learning stories
A narrative method of documenting children's learning

- They take a 'credit' rather than a 'deficit' approach.
- They recognize the unique, developing individuality of each and every learner.
- Their view of learning is holistic, not subdivided into areas, skills or aspects of learning.
- They record children's enterprises and enquiries over several days, ranging over every aspect of their experience.
- They record children's learning at home, as well as in the setting.
- They draw families in: parents find their children's stories irresistible.
- They document progression: over time, the stories get longer, broader, deeper.

FIGURE 1.7 Learning stories.

---

story, not levels, targets or goals. In New Zealand early years settings, each child's learning is documented day by day in individual books. In a New Zealand classroom, for example, Tom would have been the proud possessor of a fat volume boldly entitled 'Tom's Learning Story'. Figure 1.7 enumerates some of the key characteristics of learning stories.

These learning stories are not stored, inertly, in cupboards or filing cabinets. They are used and valued in the setting as an important resource, not least by the children themselves, who love their learning stories, and those of their friends. They carry them around the setting, they ask to have them read aloud, again and again. They often tell their educators what to write, and they contribute comments of their own about their learning. They take them home in the evenings and at weekends, for parents and grandparents to read and enjoy. It is hard to imagine children, parents or educators taking a comparable pleasure or delight in reading and re-reading a completed Foundation Stage Profile.

In this approach, it is apparent that the New Zealand educators have rejected the view that learning is momentary and discontinuous, convergent and normative, easily measured and quantified, a score, grade or level that children *have*, to varying degrees, rather than something they continuously *do*. Their construction of learning is very different; they see it as a moving event, dynamic and changeful, practically synonymous with living. They see no need to restrict their assessments to the building blocks of literacy or numeracy: the learning stories are comprehensive in their scope.

Yet more choices

The New Zealand approach has still more to teach us in our pursuit of the appropriate choices to make about the methods, purposes and outcomes of assessment. To understand its value in this part of our practice, we need to return to the four principles on which their curriculum document is founded (Ministry of Education, 1996):

- empowerment – the early childhood curriculum empowers the child to learn and grow,
- holistic development – the early childhood curriculum reflects the holistic way children learn and grow,
- family and community – the wider world of family and community is an integral part of the early childhood curriculum,
- relationships – children learn through responsive and reciprocal relationships with people, places and things.

From these principles, the Early Childhood Learning and Assessment Project derived the following four descriptors of what assessment practices are for and how they are to be shaped (Lee and Carr, 2001). They are to:

1. enhance children's sense of themselves as capable people and competent learners

2. reflect the holistic way that children learn

3. reflect the reciprocal relationships between the child, people and the learning environment

4. involve parents/guardians and, where appropriate, Whanau (extended family).

At an international early years conference in the Netherlands, where Wendy Lee, director of the Project, presented an account of their work, an overhead transparency showing these four descriptors was greeted with considerable scepticism. She was asked, with some acerbity, how she and her colleagues could possibly ensure that these fine aspirations would be realized in practice. Her reply was received in stunned silence, especially by the English delegates. She explained that these are principles enshrined in legislation. They have statutory force. There are no alternatives; the list above is not a wish list but a set of mandatory requirements. The 'Learning Stories' approach was invented to meet these requirements; as a result, in New Zealand, approaches to curriculum, to learning and to assessment are tightly aligned. They are congruent in value and in principle; the whole framework is founded on a common vision and an agreed, shared view of what children deserve. In their own words, the 'Te Whāriki' document:

> is founded on the following aspirations for children: to grow up as competent and confident learners and communicators, healthy in mind, body and spirit, secure in their sense of belonging and in the knowledge that they make a valued contribution to society.

> (Ministry of Education, 1996: 9)

In these bold statements we can see, I believe, a convincing exemplification of Professor Shipman's proposition with which I opened this chapter. Indeed, the proposition has been extended. The 'close and necessary relationship', the marriage between value and purpose, embraces both *what* the New Zealand educators assess and *how* they do it. Both are grounded in principle and value. The New Zealand educators are clear about all their choices, their choices about children (who are competent and confident learners), about learning (which is holistic, rooted in relationship) and about assessment (which is empowering, inclusive, respectful of family and community).

Where the New Zealand educators use the terms narrative and story, the educators in Reggio Emilia use the concept of pedagogical documentation. In a challenging and illuminating chapter in *In Dialogue with Reggio Emilia*, Carlina Rinaldi claims that recognizing documentation as a tool for assessment 'gives us an extremely strong "antibody" to a proliferation of assessment tools which are more and more anonymous, decontextualized and only apparently objective and democratic' (Rinaldi, 2006: 62). Her definition of the process of assessment is breathtakingly simple: 'deciding what to give value to' (Rinaldi, 2006: 70). From this definition she confidently proceeds; since assessment is, essentially, 'a perspective that gives value', it is a perspective that allows educators 'to make explicit, visible and shareable the elements of value' as they work together in the process of documentation. It is very striking, to English readers, how in this account, the responsibility of ascribing value to particular acts of learning is located firmly in the hands of the educators, who are face to face, in relationship, with the children. It is not the task of those constructing 'anonymous and decontextualized' assessment tools.

Then Rinaldi takes one marvellous step forward:

This makes the documentation particularly valuable to the children themselves, as they can encounter what they have done in the form of a narrative, seeing the meaning that the teacher has drawn from their work. In the eyes of the children, this can demonstrate that what they do has value, has meaning. So they discover that they 'exist' and can emerge from anonymity and invisibility, seeing that what they say and do is important, is listened to and is appreciated: it is a value.

(Rinaldi, 2006: 72)

This is a tremendous conclusion: children who are valued do valuable learning.

It is hard for us in England not to feel envy when we see the principled coherence and clarity of these approaches. So it is necessary to remind ourselves that the Reggio practice of documentation, and the New Zealand assessment frameworks did not drop from the heavens, whole and entire. They are the fruit of many, many years of painstaking development work, with many thousands of educators. So a more productive response than envy would be for educators here to return to the values that we hold most dear, and to act on principle in the light of those values, rather than in unwilling obedience to the prescriptions of those who promote the current standards agenda. To paraphrase and rewrite Mary Willes' insight into the lesson of obedience that children learn so early in the primary school, finding out what the Early Years Foundation Stage document, or the Primary Strategy, want us to do, and doing it, is simply not good enough. It will not result in assessment that works for children.

Conclusion

In *Learning without Limits* (2004), Susan Hart and her colleagues (of whom I am proud to be one) explore the possibility of developing an alternative improvement agenda, rooted in a rejection of the determinist assumptions of 'ability' and 'predictability' that run through our formal assessment framework like the letters in a stick of seaside rock. We argue for alternative assumptions: first, that all children are educable. We cite the powerful work of Clyde Chitty, and support his contention that:

> One of the great tragedies of the last hundred years has been our failure as a nation to take on the essential concept of human educability and thereby challenge the idea that children are born with a fixed quota of 'intelligence' which remains fixed both during childhood and adult life.
>
> (Chitty, 2001: 115)

Second, we emphasize that, as Dewey understood so well, the true aim of education is 'at every stage an added capacity for growth' (Dewey, 1916). Our alternative model of anti-determinist pedagogy replaces the concept of 'ability' and the apparatus of levels, targets and standards, with the central concept of *learning capacity*. Our case studies of nine classroom teachers suggest that a commitment to transforming learning capacity enables teachers and other educators to lift the limits that have been placed on children's learning by, amongst other things, ill-judged and unprincipled assessment practices. Furthermore, attending to the learning capacity of children and young people enables teachers to 'widen and enrich learning opportunities in such a way as to strengthen and build [children's] desire to engage and their power to further their own learning' (Hart *et al.*, 2004: 172). The nine teachers whose practice we document and analyse were equally committed to three practical, pedagogical principles: the principle of co-agency, the principle of inclusion, which we think of as 'the ethic of everybody', and the principle of trust. These principles, taken together with the concept of transforming learning capacity, would, I believe, be a profitable place from which to start on the crucial task of doing our own thinking about assessment and how we use it. We have urgent and important work to do in reconstructing, reconceptualizing and reforming the ways in which we do justice to the powerful learners with whom we work, deciding, in Rinaldi's fine words, 'what to give value to'. And it is self-evident that we cannot do that work without recourse to our own values and principles.

Points for reflection

1. To what extent do your assessment practices:
    i.   enhance children's sense of themselves as capable people and competent learners
    ii. reflect the holistic way that children learn
    iii. reflect the reciprocal relationships between the child, people and the learning environment
    iv. involve parents/guardians and, where appropriate, the extended family?
2. Rinaldi's definition of assessment is 'deciding what to give value to' (Rinaldi, 2006: 62). What do you give value to?
3. How can you be sure that your assessment practices work for children?

Further reading

Armstrong, M. (1980) *Closely Observed Children*, London: Writers and Readers.

Blenkin, G.M. and Kelly, A.V. (eds) (1992) *Assessment in Early Childhood Education*, London: Paul Chapman Publishing.

Carr, M. (2001) *Assessment in Early Childhood Settings*, London: Paul Chapman Publishing.

Drummond, M.-J. (1997) 'The uses and abuses of assessment', in C. Cullingford (ed.) *The Politics of Primary Education*, Buckingham: Open University Press.

Hart, S., Dixon, A., Drummond, M.-J. and McIntyre, D. (2004) *Learning without Limits*, Maidenhead: Open University Press.

Rinaldi, C. (2006) *In Dialogue with Reggio Emilia*, London: Routledge.

References

Adams, S., Alexander, E., Drummond, M.-J. and Moyles, J. (2004) *Inside the Foundation Stage: recreating the reception year*, London: Association of Teachers and Lecturers.

Armstrong, M. (1980) *Closely Observed Children*, London: Writers and Readers.

—— (2006) *Children Writing Stories*, Maidenhead: Open University Press.

Bensley, B. and Kilby, S. (1992) 'Induction screening', *Curriculum*, 13: 29–51.

Board of Education (1933) *Report of the Consultative Committee on Infant and Nursery Schools* (Hadow Report), London: HMSO.

CACE (Central Advisory Council on Education) (1967) *Children and their Primary Schools* (Plowden Report), London: HMSO.

Carr, M. (2001) *Assessment in Early Childhood Settings*, London: Paul Chapman Publishing.

Chitty, C. (2001) 'IQ, racism and the eugenics movement', *Forum*, 43: 115–20.

Cullingford, C. (1997) *The Politics of Primary Education*, Buckingham: Open University Press.

Dahlberg, G., Moss, P. and Pence, A. (1999) *Beyond Quality in Early Childhood and Care: postmodern perspectives*, London: Falmer Press.

Dewey, J. (1916) *Democracy and Education*, New York: Macmillan.

DfES (2007) *Statutory Framework for the Early Years Foundation Stage*, London: DfES.

Drummond, M.-J. (2003) *Assessing Children's Learning* (2nd edn), London: David Fulton.

Drummond, M.-J., Rouse, D. and Pugh, G. (1992) *Making Assessment Work: values and principles in assessing children's learning*, Nottingham: NES Arnold in association with the National Children's Bureau.

Edwards, C., Gandini, L. and Forman, G. (eds) (1993) *The Hundred Languages of Children: the Reggio Emilia approach to early childhood education*, Norwood, NJ: Ablex.

Hart, S., Dixon, A., Drummond, M.-J. and McIntyre, D. (2004) *Learning without Limits*, Maidenhead: Open University Press.

Isaacs, S. (1930) *Intellectual Growth in Young Children*, London: Routledge and Kegan Paul.

—— (1933) *Social Development in Young Children*, London: Routledge.

James, M., Black, P., Carmichael, P., Drummond, M.-J., Fox, A., MacBeath, J., Marshall, B., McCormick, R., Pedder, D., Procter, R., Swaffield, S., Swann, J., and Wiliam, D. (2007) *Improving Learning How to Learn: classrooms, schools and networks*, London: Routledge.

Lee, W. and Carr, M. (2001) 'Learning stories as an assessment tool for early childhood', Paper presented at the 11th European Conference on Quality in Early Childhood Education, EECERA Conference, Alkmaar, the Netherlands.

Ministry of Education (1996) *Te Whāriki Early Childhood Curriculum*, Wellington, New Zealand: Learning Media.

Moss, P. and Petrie, P. (2002) *From Children's Services to Children's Spaces*, London: RoutledgeFalmer.

QCA (Qualifications and Curriculum Authority) (2000) *Curriculum Guidance for the Foundation Stage*, London: DfES/QCA.

—— (2003) *Foundation Stage Profile*, London: QCA.

Rinaldi, C. (2006) *In Dialogue with Reggio Emilia*, London: Routledge.

Tobin, J.J., Wu, D. and Davidson, D. (1989) *Preschool in Three Cultures*, New Haven: Yale University Press.

Willes, M. (1983) *Children into Pupils*, London: Routledge and Kegan Paul.

Assessment and learning

Mary James

Can three generations of assessment practice be housed under the same roof or is inter-generational conflict inevitable?

Introduction

Little words matter. In the chapters that follow this one, you will find that the little words 'of', 'for' and 'as' are used to highlight particular kinds of relationships between 'assessment' and 'learning'. The job of this chapter is to prepare the ground for these more detailed accounts by examining the links between assessment 'and' learning in general terms.

The main thrust of my argument is that assessments need to be congruent with our views of learning if they are to be valid – a crucial condition for trust being placed upon them. Some assessments carried out in schools do not claim to assess learning (a point I shall return to below) but, for the most part, teachers are concerned with assessments linked to learning and it is important to think carefully about what this means. In particular, I encourage you to ask how well any assessment is aligned with the kind of learning undertaken by students because experience suggests that quite often they are out of sync.

In recent years our understanding of how people learn has been developing apace as a result of applying concepts and methods from a range of different fields of research: from anthropology to neuroscience. However, developments in assessment have often been more dependent on advances in measurement technologies, especially those, such as e-assessment techniques, that might enhance the reliability, manageability and security of large-scale testing programmes. The problem is that the latter tend to take insufficient account of the most recent developments in learning theory. Equally, researchers developing learning theory rarely work out the full implications of their ideas for assessment practice. In consequence it is often teachers, in the context of their need to make assessment decisions in classrooms, who are left to ask two vital questions:

1.   To what extent do the assessments available to me, or which I create, reflect the kind of learning that I aim to promote in students?

2.   If assessments lack congruence with learning, how can I try to bring them into closer alignment?

I outline below what I call three generations of ideas about links between assessment and learning and their implications. Here I adapt some headings developed by Chris Watkins (2003) as descriptions of different views of learning:

- learning is being taught
- learning is individual sense-making
- learning is building knowledge as part of doing things with others.

Although these ideas co-exist, especially in current assessment practice, I have called them generations, because, like generations within families, they were born and came to maturity at different points in history, although they share some heritage and association.

First generation assessment practice: assessing learning of what is taught

Two different sets of assumptions underpin this generation of assessment practices but both share a preoccupation with what is taught, and how well knowledge is transmitted and absorbed by learners. Learning is regarded largely as the acquisition of what the teacher or trainer wants to teach and little attention is paid to whether, or how, this knowledge might be modified in the process. Thus learners are regarded as rather passive and success is judged by the extent to which they acquire the knowledge and reproduce the behaviours that the teacher intended.

'Folk' views of learning

The first set of assumptions is not based on any evidence-informed theory of learning at all, but rather a 'folk' psychology that regards the brain or mind (the two are not always clearly distinguished) as a kind of vessel or sponge into which information is poured. Learning is assumed to have occurred when this knowledge is 'retained'.

Perhaps the most explicit expression of this view is found in Charles Dickens' novel, *Hard Times*, in which Gradgrind describes children's minds as like little pitchers to be filled full of facts. The job of the teachers is therefore to know a lot of facts and tell them to pupils whose job it is to memorize them. Although this is a caricature, there are still a lot of people who hold something like this view, especially among those who are not education professionals. If teachers need to convince lay people, such as parents, that learning is more complicated, they may need to take such assumptions into account when trying to communicate a more sophisticated view.

Of course, learning does involve memory. Eric Kandel (2006), who won a Nobel Prize for his research on memory, emphasizes how much memory matters to our sense of being human with a quote from Tennessee Williams: 'Has it ever struck you … that life is all memory, except for the one present moment that goes by so quickly that you hardly catch it going?' So, remembering things is fundamental. What is much more questionable is that pupils should, or can, remember things in exactly the same way as they are remembered by their teachers. As we shall see later in this chapter, the idea that it is possible to achieve one to one correspondence between what is in the teacher's head and what the pupil learns is neither realistic nor ultimately desirable. Nevertheless, clear communication and explanation by teachers are crucial to children's learning (Ted Wragg considered his work on explaining to be his most important, see Wragg and Brown, 2001a, b) as is their ability to inspire enthusiasm for their subject. These are attributes continually referred to in the 'My Best Teacher' column of *The Times Educational Supplement*. Recognition of the truth that teachers need to be able to impart knowledge also contributed to the success of Alan Bennett's portrayal of Hector in his play *The History Boys*. In a *Guardian* review of the play (19 May 2004), Michael Billington wrote:

> Clearly Bennett is writing in praise of Hector and the non-utilitarian, anti-Gradgrind approach to education. At the same time, he is fair enough to show that in history, above all, you need a certain grounding in facts before you can begin to achieve interpretation.

The point of this is to emphasize that we need not be against the memorization of facts and information if we nevertheless want to argue for a more complex and nuanced view of learning.

Behaviourist views of learning

Arguably a more reductionist view derives from the second set of assumptions that I alluded to earlier. Unlike the folk psychology of both Gradgrind and Hector, these assumptions are based on research evidence but within a tradition that has fallen out of favour. Behaviourism is its name. This perspective was derived from a concern to develop a proper science of human behaviour based on observation and experiment. Mental processes are not directly observable so they were excluded from investigation. Indeed, many behaviourists claimed that there is 'no ghost in the machine' because they believed that even consciousness could be reduced to physical processes.

The basic tenet of behaviourism is that learning can be viewed as conditioned response to external stimuli. In other words, if a particular stimulus produces a response, the recurrence of the stimulus, or something closely associated with it, will cause the response to be repeated. In Pavlov's dogs, the presentation of food caused them to salivate but, over time, after repeated occasions when the food was presented whilst a bell was rung, the ringing of a bell alone caused them to salivate. Applied to human learning, this theory has been used successfully in situations where a particular behavioural response is sought. Rewards and punishments, or more commonly the withholding of rewards, 'condition' desired responses. Repetition of the stimulus makes the response habitual; hence the value of repeated practice. Eventually the response is so automatic that it can be produced at speed.

These ideas may sound somewhat old-fashioned today. However, whilst theory has moved on, practice stemming from it has persisted, and sometimes for good reason. There are times when it is legitimate to expect people to learn to behave in particular ways, instantly, and without worrying too much about the whys and wherefores. As every parent knows, there are times when a repeated instruction, the sharp rebuke, or non-specific praise elicits a behaviour that keeps a child safe – from falling under a car, for instance. Furthermore, in a world where there is so much to know and understand, individuals have to make strategic judgements about what they want to understand in depth and what they will be content to know only 'on the surface' or as a conditioned response. And this may vary from person to person and context to context. For example, a basic level of functional numeracy might be adequate for the aspiring artist, but not for the aspiring engineer.

As with the folk psychology, described above, rote learning is associated with the behaviourist approach but there are other features as well. For example, behaviourism assumes that a complex skill can be taught by being broken down into components, each of which can be taught separately then reassembled. Another assumption is that if an idea or practice is common to many contexts, it is most economical to teach it separately, in abstraction, so that it can then be applied in many situations. Moreover, it is considered best to learn basic facts and skills first on which more sophisticated knowledge and practice can later be built.

Implications for assessment

The assumptions and beliefs about learning outlined above, lead to equivalent assumptions about the kinds of assessments that are most appropriate. Characteristically, assessment in first generation assessment practice might have all or some, of the following features.

- The learning of the individual is assessed and any evidence that performance on a test or assessment is influenced by others is regarded as cheating.
- The focus is on performance under test conditions.
- Performance tends to be defined as demonstration of ability to recall facts and information, or to demonstrate skills, i.e. showing what the learner knows and can do.
- Tests or tasks are specially constructed for the purpose of assessment and are scheduled at the end of a course or sequence of learning; they are regarded as separate from learning.
- Preparation for tests may involve practice, for example by using past papers, but results on these will not count towards a grade, etc.
- Tests are time limited, on the assumption that speed of completion of the tasks indicates that the learning is well established.
- No access to materials is allowed other than those needed to do the immediate task because the knowledge or skill is expected to be memorized or established as a competence.
- Questions or tasks for completion are organized in a hierarchy of difficulty, starting with the least difficult, often in the form of short answer or multiple choice items.
- Responses or performances are assessed as correct or incorrect and results from a test are aggregated to give a score enabling comparison with other learners (norm-referenced), against a standard (criterion-referenced) or against the learner's own previous performance (ipsative-referenced). Sometimes these referencing systems are combined, e.g. norm with criterion referencing (see the chapter by Pete Dudley and Sue Swaffield in this volume for a more detailed discussion of these forms of comparison).
- It may be possible to infer areas for improvement (where incorrect responses were made) from returned marked scripts, if these are available, but rarely from global scores. Global scores only indicate that a learner has done well or should try to do better. However, tightly structured, interactive computer-based assessments can direct the test-taker back to an easier level of performance, during an assessment, if he or she fails at a particular level.

The remarkable thing about this list is how familiar it has become. Indeed, many lay people would probably take it for granted that these are characteristics of all tests and assessments, which suggests that folk and behaviourist assumptions are still very prevalent in our culture. Below, I outline other possible approaches which are better aligned with rather different views about learning.

Points for reflection

Think about assessments that you have encountered as a student, parent or professional. Collect examples if possible, such as recent SAT tests, GCSE exam papers or vocational assessments. Create a checklist from the characteristics given above and tick those characteristics that these assessments possess. Are there differences among the examples? What might these indicate about the views of assessment and learning that the assessments embody?

Second generation assessment practice: assessing learning as individual sense-making

This generation of assessment practices is similar to the first generation in that it continues to focus on the individual and acquisition of knowledge and skill, but it takes a more active view of learning and recognizes that what is learnt is rarely identical to what is taught. An emphasis on individual meaning-making indicates a particular interest in cognition: the working of the mind as a function of the brain. Assessments, from this viewpoint, go beyond testing factual recall to tap into deeper understandings.

Cognitive constructivist views of learning

Behaviourists' denial of the importance of mental processes in learning provoked a reaction from psychologists, linguists, cognitive scientists, computer scientists and, latterly, neuroscientists, who were quick to point out that learning must, at the very least, involve thinking. All argued that learning is determined largely by what goes on in people's heads. More significantly, however, they argued that learning involves people in making sense of the world by building mental models of how the world works so that they can interpret – or make sense of – new information. Thus learning is not simply absorbing information but an active process of meaning-making.

There is currently much talk of 'personalised learning' but, according to the cognitive constructivist view, learning is by definition personalised because people will always make sense of their experiences in unique ways. No one person's mental models will be quite the same as those of others because they have been shaped by different prior experiences. These models provide the lenses through which we view new experiences and lead us to pay great attention to some features and perhaps ignore others. Generally this is useful to us because these selections of what is worth attending to help us to manage the quantity of incoming sensory data. Indeed, one of the possible explanations why some people on the autistic spectrum can, for example, recall and draw the detail of complicated building structures, is because they do not possess the mental filters that most of us have. They attend to everything rather than a selection of data determined by conceptions of what is salient. Of course, such frameworks can also blind us to the significance of new experiences – even lead us to adopt prejudiced views. In this context the task of teaching is not simply to impart information, or to provide practice for skill development, but to help learners evaluate established mental maps and adapt, extend or renew them so that they expand perception and deepen understanding.

The emphasis within this perspective is on the development of conceptual understanding, which is particularly important in the learning of academic subjects. Thus 'concepts', and the relationships among them, are significant because these form the basis of our mental models (schema). The need to build such models is familiar in schools, from the use of 'spider diagrams' to map topics in primary schools, to concept mapping as revision practice in secondary schools. At a simple level the nodes in these diagrams are usually nouns and the links are verbs.

Such models are built using a range of mental processes. Acquiring knowledge is one such process but at a higher (or deeper) level are processes such as comprehension, application, analysis, synthesis and evaluation – categories derived from Benjamin Bloom's (1956) influential classification of cognitive objectives. The application of concepts in solving problems is particularly valued for its capacity to reveal understanding and to lead to the construction of new knowledge. Failures to solve problems can often be traced to misunderstandings of concepts or their relationships. For example, understandings or misunderstanding of the nature and role of photosynthesis in plants can have profound consequences for solving problems of climate change.

The task for education, according to this view, is to help novices acquire the ways of thinking possessed by experts, notably the ways they organize knowledge so that it is more retrievable and useful. Characteristically, experts solve problems more quickly, with 'less search', because their models help them to know what is relevant. They are also capable of reflecting upon and controlling their mental processes through the exercise of metacognitive processes – thinking about thinking.

Implications for assessment

Some of the implications for assessment practice that flow from cognitive constructivist views of learning are similar to those of the first generation, above, but there are also significant differences in approach and emphasis. Thus, assessment in second generation assessment practices might have all or some, of the following features.

- Again, the learning of the individual is assessed.
- But, the focus is on problem solving and understanding.
- Performance tends to be defined as demonstration of ability to apply conceptual frameworks to find solutions to problems, and to demonstrate cognitive skills.
- Tests and examinations are specially constructed for the purpose of assessment and are often scheduled at the end of a course or sequence of learning.
- Tasks may be extended in order to allow those being assessed to display the breadth and depth of their understanding, or to solve complex problems. Thus, essays, concept maps, think-aloud protocols, open-ended assignments, projects, coursework or theses may be the preferred form of response.
- Assessments are, nevertheless, often time limited, on the assumption that speed of completion indicates that acquisition of conceptual models promote understanding and problem solving with 'less search'.
- Some limited access to materials, such as the text of novels or poetry in literature examinations, may be permitted because the assessment is less a test of memory than an assessment of understanding.
- Responses to the tasks or problems are assessed according to specified criteria, which involve judgement on the part of the assessor because there will rarely be one correct answer. Assessors therefore need to be trained to ensure that their assessments are in agreement with those of others. They may be given access to marking schemes (what Americans call 'scoring rubrics') and exemplars (or model answers) for this purpose. Within schools this will probably require the setting up of moderation procedures so that teachers can share and discuss their judgements of a selection of work, thus developing a conception of appropriate standards in a progression from novice to expert.
- The notion of a progression often implies a ladder of scores, levels or grades based on some norm-referenced assumptions, i.e. that a normal trajectory of progress can be described.
- Another assumption is that improvement comes from efforts to close the gap between novice and expert performance. This need not be interpreted as a linear progression but could be regarded as development towards a horizon of possibilities.
- Areas for improvement can be inferred from misunderstandings or failures to find viable solutions to problems. These may indicate flawed conceptual understanding or poor frameworks that need to be revisited, unpicked and reconstructed. This implies that certain ideas may need to be unlearned or relearned in formative classroom processes, or that new cognitive skills need to be developed

This second generation of assessment practices, like the first generation, remain focused on the acquisition and processing of knowledge, as something ultimately 'possessed' by individuals. For this reason, some tests or examinations combine elements of both behaviourist and constructivist approaches. Tests that begin with short answer questions based on factual recall, progressing to more extended problem-solving tasks or essay-type questions, might be examples.

Points for reflection: metaphors of learning

The metaphors people use when talking about learning are very revealing of the way they think about it. Look back over this chapter: how many metaphors can you find? Thus far, discussion here has been dominated by metaphors that imply that learning is a commodity – acquired, retained and possessed by individuals. Learning as meaning-making through knowledge construction has also appeared, although this has also been discussed as a property of individuals. Over a period of, say, one week, make a collection of other metaphors of learning you come across and make a note of who said them, and in what context. Politicians, journalists, parents, teachers and children could all be sources. What do these metaphors tell you about different perspectives?

Anna Sfard (1998) points out that underpinning discussions about how people learn are two key metaphors: a metaphor of acquisition and a metaphor of participation. Broadly speaking, folk theories, behaviourist theories and constructivist theories are concerned with the individual's acquisition of skills, knowledge and understanding, whilst socio-cultural theories, which we come to next, see learning as embodied in and through participation in social and cultural activity.

However, there is at least one more metaphor for learning that is important, particularly if we value creativity and innovation as a goal of learning. Teachers of creative subjects, for instance, often aim for learners to go beyond the acquisition of skills, knowledge, understanding and dispositions, or learning how to practise as experts have before them. They hope that their students will produce something novel or original. Thus 'knowledge creation' can be viewed as learning too (Paavola et al., 2004); indeed it is the key criterion for the award of PhDs.

Metaphors help us to look at learning in different ways and to challenge our taken-for-granted assumptions. However, Sfard cautions against showing too great a devotion to one particular metaphor. Although some people might argue that the different views are logically incompatible, teachers will probably use mixed metaphors quite happily.

The third generation of assessment practice (below) makes a more radical shift – away from seeing learning as acquisition of knowledge and/or understanding to learning as participation in social practices.

Third generation assessment practice: assessing learning as building knowledge as part of doing things with others

This generation of assessment practice is based on what, as mentioned in the box above, is often called the socio-cultural, or 'situated', perspective on learning. It is sometimes regarded as a new development because it is currently enjoying popularity amongst academics and researchers. However, Bredo (1997) traces its intellectual origins back to the work of William James, John Dewey and George Herbert Mead at the beginning of the twentieth century. Its origins therefore pre-date both behaviourism and cognitive constructivism. Indeed, James Watson, the principal evangelist of behaviourism, was a student of Dewey at the University of Chicago but admitted that he never understood him.

The socio-cultural view of learning

A key principle of socio-cultural theory is that learning involves both thought and action in context and is particularly influenced by the interactions among these phenomena. This may explain why it is often seen as more complex than behaviourism, which concentrates on behaviour, or cognitivism, which focuses on thought processes. The 'interactionist' approach of Dewey and Mead viewed human development as a transaction between the individual and the environment (actor and structure). This had something in common with the development of cultural psychology in Russia, associated with Vygotsky (1978), who was himself influenced by William James, and possibly met Dewey. This transatlantic 'conversation', as it were, continued as Vygotsky's thinking subsequently influenced theorists such as Bruner (1996) in the USA and Engeström (1999) in Finland. Other key theorists who regard individual learning as 'situated' in the social environment include Barbara Rogoff (1990), Jean Lave and Etienne Wenger (Lave and Wenger, 1991; Wenger, 1998), who draw on anthropological work to characterize learning as 'cognitive apprenticeship' in 'communities of practice'.

Given the intellectual roots – deriving as much from social theory, sociology and anthropology as from psychology – the language, concepts and metaphors employed in socio-cultural approaches are often quite distinct. For example, 'agency', 'community', 'rules', 'roles', 'division of labour', 'artefacts' and 'contradictions' feature prominently.

According to this perspective, thinking is conducted through actions that alter the situation and the situation changes the thinking; the two constantly interact. Especially important is the notion that learning is a mediated activity in which cultural tools and artefacts have a crucial role. These can be physical artefacts such as books and equipment but they can be symbolic tools such as language and sign systems. Since language, which is central to our capacity to think, is developed in relationships between people, social relationships are necessary for learning. Learning is by definition a social and collaborative activity in which people build knowledge and develop their thinking together.

Learning involves participation and what is learned is not the property of an individual but distributed within the social group. For example, an ability to use language skills is not solely an indication of individual intelligence but of the intelligence of the community that developed the language, which the individual then puts to use. Thus the collective knowledge of the group or community is internalized by the individual. Similarly, as an individual creates new knowledge, for example, a new way of using a tool, then he or she will externalize that knowledge in communicating it to others who will put it to use and then internalize it. Therefore, knowledge is created and shared in expansive learning cycles. Within the Learning How to Learn project (see James *et al.*, 2006: Part IV) we saw examples of this as teachers developed and shared ideas associated with assessment for learning practices, such as the use of 'traffic lights'.

These ideas have implications for teaching. They imply that the teacher needs to create an environment in which people can be stimulated to think and act in authentic tasks (like apprentices) beyond their current level of competence (but in what Vygotsky calls their zone of proximal development). Access to, and use of, an appropriate range of tools is an important aspect of such an expansive learning environment. It is important to find activities that a learner can complete with assistance but not alone so that the 'more expert other', in some cases the teacher but often a peer, can 'scaffold' their learning and remove the scaffold when they can cope on their own. Tasks need to be collaborative and students need to be involved both in the generation of problems and of solutions. Teachers and students become a community and jointly solve problems, so all develop their skill and understanding.

According to this view, the most valued outcomes of learning are therefore engaged participation in ways that others in the community of practice find beneficial. It follows that it is problematic to judge an individual as having acquired knowledge in general terms, i.e. abstracted from action settings.

Implications for assessment

These socio-cultural theories provide powerful descriptions and explanations of learning but their implications for assessment, especially in school contexts, have not been fully worked out. This is not really surprising because the key theorists have focused on learning, rather than assessment. However, if assessment is to be aligned with learning then appropriate linkages need to be found. The pointers for third generation assessment practices that follow are therefore somewhat speculative and are my attempt to extrapolate from the theory.

- If learning cannot be separated from the actions in which it is embodied, then assessment too must be 'situated'. This implies that assessment is carried out alongside learning, not as an 'after learning' event.
- Assessment alongside learning implies that it needs to be done by the community rather than by external assessors. Thus there is a role for self-assessment, peer assessment and teacher assessment.
- Assessment of group learning is as important as the learning of the individual.
- *In vivo* studies of complex, situated problem solving are the most appropriate form for assessments to take because learning is expressed in participation in authentic (real-world) activities or projects.
- The focus is on how well people exercise 'agency' in their use of the resources or tools (intellectual, human, material) available to them to formulate problems, work productively and evaluate their efforts. This is a proper justification for course-work assignments and encourages access to source materials because it is the way that these are used that is of most significance.
- Learning outcomes can be captured and reported through various forms of recording, including narrative accounts and audio and visual media.
- The portfolio has an important role because it has the potential to capture 'assessment as inquiry'. However, attempts to 'grade' portfolios according to 'scoring rubrics', as has happened in the USA, is out of alignment with the socio-cultural perspective because it reduces the possibilities to 'assessment as procedure' or even 'assessment as measurement' (Serafini, 2000).
- Judgement needs to be holistic and qualitative, to be consistent with a socio-cultural or situated approach, not atomized and quantified as in measurement approaches.

This list of characteristics of third generation assessment practices points to possibilities for forms of assessment in sympathy with valued teaching and learning practices in schools and workplaces. It is especially suited to the assessment of collaborative group work on extended projects. This could make it especially attractive to employers who increasingly claim they are interested in recruits who can demonstrate their capability to work in teams to find creative solutions to complex problems. However, it raises questions about how to ensure the trust-worthiness of such assessments when large numbers of students are involved and when those who are interested in the outcomes of such learning cannot partici-pate in the activities that generate them. The apprenticeship model, on which some of these ideas are built, may offer some solutions because underpinning such models is the concept of the guild that is the guardian and arbiter of devel-oping standards. In other words, validation of standards by a community of experts (like master craftsmen) may be a way of assuring quality. Within UK vocational education, systems of internal and external assessors and verifiers have attempted to do this although large-scale systems almost inevitably become bureaucratic, unwieldy and reductive. Clearly, more work needs to be done to develop approaches to assessment that are coherent with socio-cultural perspec-tives on learning.

Points for reflection

Reflect on your own experience, and try to identify examples of assessments that approximate to this third generation of assessment practice. Consider informal classroom assessment as well as formal assessments, vocational assess-ments as well as academic assessments, and assessments of adults as well as of children. In what ways might these practices need to be adapted to bring them more in line with the socio-cultural view of learning? What would you expect the barriers to implementation to be, for example selling the idea to a sceptical public, and how might they be overcome? Would it be worth the effort?

A note on assessments that do not claim to focus on learning

At the beginning of this chapter, I noted that some forms of assessment found in schools do not claim to assess learning. Instead of assessing current achievement, they are intended to predict future performance or to identify students who possess certain mental traits or faculties, and who might benefit from special pro-vision. The former are often called 'aptitude tests' and the latter 'ability tests'.

Although current expansion in specialist schools encourages some selection by aptitude, aptitude tests are not much used in schools and choice of a specialism depends more on other measures such as teacher report, prior achievements or expressions of interest. In the workplace, however, employers are more inclined to use tests of such things as adaptability, leadership, teamwork, goal-orientation, which they especially value.

Tests of putative mental traits, especially cognitive ability, are however common in schools. These assume that differences can be detected in the 'natural' endowment of individuals. In some senses this is a peculiarly Western obsession because Asian–Pacific countries with a Confucian heritage are much more interested in the contribution of effort to success.

Again, cognitive ability tests are valued for their predictive validity: their capacity to predict future performance if the environment for learning is conducive. They are constructed so that the assessment of current learning achievement is minimized although learning cannot be screened out altogether because, for instance, students need to be able to read, recognize symbols or understand spoken language in order to interpret the questions asked. However there are technical ways of taking account of these learning effects, and other effects associated with age, gender and cultural differences. Apart from persuasive marketing by the organizations that produce them, current widespread use of cognitive ability tests in schools is attributable to concerns to identify students who may be underachieving in formal assessments of achievement, such as SATs and GCSE examinations. Such information can then assist decisions about the kinds of support that groups or individuals need in order to fulfil their potential. That is the rhetoric, but whether they are used in this way is sometimes more questionable.

Points for reflection

Do you have experience of the use of aptitude or ability tests, either in your personal or professional life? How were they used? Was this use consistent with their assumptions and purpose? Were they valuable? Did their use contribute to learning in the short, medium or long term?

Conclusion

This chapter has attempted to show what consistency between assessment practice and beliefs about learning might look like. However, assessment practice is sometimes out of line. This can undermine effective teaching and learning because assessment 'washback' is so powerful, especially in high stakes settings. It is therefore worth trying to achieve a better alignment between assessment, teaching and learning. A key question for teachers and assessors is whether they can blend approaches or whether they need to adopt a particular approach to the exclusion of others. Can all three generations of assessment practice be housed under the same roof or is inter-generational conflict inevitable?

As in households, the answer is probably 'yes and no' but pragmatic compromises can sometimes be reached so that all live in relative harmony. The overarching principle for peaceful co-existence is likely to be 'fitness for purpose': always a key criterion for choice of assessments. For example, behaviourist approaches seem to work perfectly well when the focus is on the development of some basic skills or habitual behaviours. In these contexts, too much thought might actually get in the way of performance: if you think about how to ride a bicycle you are likely to fall off. Cognitivist approaches seem to work well when deep understanding of conceptual structures within subject domains is the desired outcome.

The nature of the subject domain might also encourage one approach in preference to another. For example, science and mathematics, with hierarchically ordered conceptual structures may lend themselves to constructivist approaches better than broader 'fields' of study, such as the expressive arts, with contested or multiple criteria of what counts as quality learning. The latter may sit better with socio-cultural approaches, which value context, process and community.

However, there is evidence that learning theory is shifting from former paradigmatic stances. Many constructivists have taken on board the importance of the social dimension of learning: hence the increasing use of the term 'social constructivism'. And socio-culturalists are involved in a 'discursive shift' to recognize the cognitive potential to explain how we learn new practices (Edwards, 2005). This suggests possibilities for synthesis whereby a more complete theory can emerge from blending and bonding of key elements of previous theories. Such synthesis may lead to a new alignment. The possibility for a more complete and inclusive theory of learning to guide the practice of teaching and assessment seems to be a goal worth pursuing.

Points for reflection

Look back over the three lists of assessment characteristics and compare and contrast them. Is there scope for an integrated model, or are some of the characteristics so opposed that only a choice between them would be possible?

What different learning contexts, in your experience, would favour the different approaches?

Further reading

Bransford, J.D., Brown, A.L. and Cocking, R. (eds) (2000) *How People Learn: brain, mind, experience, and school*, Washington, DC: National Academy Press.

Pellegrino, J.W., Chudowsky, N. and Glaser, R. (eds) (2001) *Knowing What Students Know: the science and design of educational assessment*, Washington, DC: National Academy Press.

Watkins, C. (2003) *Learning: a sense-maker's guide*, London: Association of Teachers and Lecturers.

References

Bloom, B.S. (ed.) (1956) *Taxonomy of Educational Objectives, the classification of educational goals – handbook I: cognitive domain*, New York: McKay.

Bredo, E. (1997) 'The social construction of learning', in G.D. Phye (ed.) *Handbook of Academic Learning: construction of knowledge*, San Diego, CA: Academic Press.

Bruner, J. (1996) *The Culture of Education*, Cambridge, MA: Harvard University Press.

Edwards, A. (2005) 'Let's get beyond community and practice: the many meanings of learning by participating', *Curriculum Journal*, 16: 49–65.

Engeström, Y. (1999) 'Activity theory and individual and social transformation', in Y. Engeström, R. Miettinen and R.-L. Punamäki (eds) *Perspectives on Activity Theory*, Cambridge: Cambridge University Press.

James, M., Black, P., Carmichael, P., Conner, C., Dudley, P., Fox, A., Frost, D., Honour, L., MacBeath, J., McCormick, R., Marshall, B., Pedder, D., Procter, R., Swaffield, S. and Wiliam, D. (2006) *Learning How to Learn: tools for schools*, London: Routledge.

Kandel, E. (2006) *In Search of Memory: the emergence of a new science of mind*, New York: Norton.

Lave, J. and Wenger, E. (1991) *Situated Learning: legitimate peripheral participation*, Cambridge: Cambridge University Press.

Paavola, S., Lipponen, L. and Hakkarainen, K. (2004) 'Models of innovative knowledge communities and three metaphors of learning', *Review of Educational Research*, 74: 557–76.

Rogoff, B. (1990) *Apprenticeship in Thinking: cognitive development in social context*, New York: Oxford University Press.

Serafini, F. (2000) 'Three paradigms of assessment: measurement, procedure, and inquiry', *Reading Teacher*, 54: 384–93.

Sfard, A. (1998) 'On two metaphors for learning and the dangers of choosing just one', *Educational Researcher*, 27: 4–13.

Vygotsky, L.S. (1978) *Mind in Society: the development of higher psychological process*, Cambridge, MA: Harvard University Press.

Watkins, C. (2003) *Learning: a sense-maker's guide*, London: Association of Teachers and Lecturers.

Wenger, E. (1998) *Communities of Practice*, Cambridge: Cambridge University Press.

Wragg, E.C. and Brown, G. (2001a) *Explaining in the Primary School*, London: RoutledgeFalmer.

—— (2001b) *Explaining in the Secondary School*, London: RoutledgeFalmer.

Can assessment unlock and open the doors to resourcefulness and agency?

Margaret Carr

Intelligence in the wild includes the ability to recognize problems hidden in messy situations and the motivation and good sense to choose which problems (because there are always too many!) are worth the time and the energy it will take to solve them.

(Perkins, 2000: 1)

Introduction

This chapter raises some questions about assessment practices when learning outcomes are fuzzy and learning settings are messy: when learning is 'in the wild', as David Perkins suggests. Classrooms and early childhood settings are examples of 'wild' and complex contexts that 'present a wilderness of vaguely marked and ill-defined occasions for thoughtful engagement' (Perkins *et al.*, 2000: 270). Solving problems, taking action and interacting with others in these contexts calls for more than knowledge and abilities. The inclination to 'follow through' on intentions, and the capacity to notice, recognize, use and create opportunities to do so, are also key requirements. An abilities-centric view of intelligent performance can prevail in a testing situation or a worksheet where the task is prescribed and the criteria for success are clearly marked, but interesting situations are not usually like this and, as Perkins and his colleagues point out, the task of exercising one's intelligence 'in the wild' is 'strikingly different'. Assessment in the wild calls for complex analysis that includes interpretation and recognition of significant events and opportunities. This is true for both teachers and learners. Perhaps some classrooms are less wild than others, but an appropriate, and indeed, an urgent, educational task is to assist young people to be prepared for the diversity of twenty-first century wildernesses that they will encounter, as well as to learn in the complex situations of their current lives.

Learning dispositions

Learning dispositions are educational outcomes that combine knowledge and abilities with other attributes like inclination and sensitivity to occasion (Perkins *et al.*, 1993). They are often 'fuzzy'; their shape is indistinct, their boundaries are unclear and their scope is uncertain. But they turn ability into action (Ritchhart, 2002: 18) and they are useful in the wild. There is a considerable literature about them and what they look like in different places. Gordon Wells comments, for instance, in the context of research on inquiry as an orientation for learning, on 'the dispositions of caring, collaboration and critical inquiry [that] are at the heart of our vision of education' (Wells, 2002: 205). Learning dispositions are part of a family of outcomes that have been variously called intellectual habits (Sizer, 1992), mindsets (Dweck, 1999), patterns of strategic action (Pollard and Filer, 1999), habits of mind (Costa and Kallick, 2000), thinking dispositions (Perkins *et al.*, 1993; Ritchhart, 2002), learning dispositions (Carr, 2001a) and learning power (Claxton, 2002). Guy Claxton and I have suggested we might consider them as verbs:

> We suggest that, when we look at what value these ideas of 'life-long' learning might have for teachers in early childhood settings and schools, there is merit in reading 'disposition' not as a noun, as a 'thing' to be acquired, but as a verb with qualifying adverbs. One does not 'acquire a disposition', one becomes more or less 'disposed' to respond in such-and-such a way.
>
> (Claxton and Carr, 2004: 88)

They are about being ready willing and able to learn, and might be defined as 'participation repertoires from which a learner recognizes, selects, edits, responds to, resists, searches for and constructs learning opportunities' (Carr, 2001a: 10).

Learning dispositions and 'life-long' learning

Learning dispositions, as harbingers of 'life-long' learning, are assumed to cross the contexts of subject areas, places and to develop over time, but the transfer of learning is a vexed topic, and learning dispositions are 'renowned for failures to achieve transfer' (Bereiter, 1995: 22). This is an area where imaginative research and theoretical frameworks are providing insights (for instance Bereiter, 1995; Bransford and Schwartz, 1999; Tuomi-Gröhn and Engeström, 2003). Carl Bereiter (and other writers as well, e.g. Greeno *et al.*, 1996; Perkins *et al.*, 1993; Ritchhart, 2002) emphasizes the value of students being 'well attuned to the variety of life's situations' (Bereiter, 1995: 24) in order for learning dispositions to transfer. Similarly, Sasha Barab and Wolff-Michael Roth describe learning dispositions and the skills and knowledges that are associated with them as 'the attunements and behaviours that an individual can enlist to realize an affordance network' (Barab and Roth, 2006: 3): a network of useful resources, including people, that provide, or appear to provide, opportunities and constraints for the learning that the individual has in mind.

Longitudinal research studies have therefore contributed particularly usefully to the literature on learning dispositions and similar outcomes. The most well known of these studies in recent times is the longitudinal research of Andrew Pollard and Ann Filer (Pollard and Filer, 1996, 1999; Filer and Pollard, 2000). The authors concluded that children's social development can be conceptualized in terms of 'strategic biography', and that, over time, characteristic patterns of strategic action and orientation to learning tend to become established. Parents, particularly mothers, played a significant role in discussing, mediating and helping to interpret new experiences and new challenges. They conclude that changing power relations in a setting may enhance or threaten a child's established sense of self as a pupil and 'existing strategies are liable to modification or change if they become no longer viable, appropriate or comfortable for a pupil to maintain' (Pollard and Filer, 1999: 304). The authors' concept of 'pupil career' 'reflects the year-by-year interplay of previous orientations and contextually specific forms of strategic actions in schools. It has particular consequences in terms of identity, self-confidence and learning disposition' (Pollard and Filer, 1999: 304).

How adults perceive the outcomes of education can influence the effect of early childhood experience in early years settings. In a longitudinal ethnographic study in New Zealand, Sally Peters (2004) followed the progress of seven case study children and their families, from the children's last months in early childhood education, when they were four years old, until the children were eight and had been at school for three years. The author describes the transition to school as the border between different 'cultures'. The 'dispositions, resources and demand characteristics' of the case study children interacted with features of the environment that appeared to inhibit, permit or invite engagement. Deficit approaches, assessed by a list of basic skills, were in some cases a major focus for intervention at school, overshadowing much of the child's previous experience. There is a parallel here with a model of 'life cycle skill formation': orientations and dispositions build on earlier orientations and dispositions to develop an evolving sense of self, while the 'investment' in this learning in successive contexts (the power relations and assessment methods, for instance) are significant influences (Cunha et al., 2005).

Learning dispositions are described as important outcomes in the New Zealand national early childhood curriculum, Te Whāriki.

An example of a learning disposition is the disposition to be curious. It may be characterized by: an inclination to enjoy puzzling over events; the skills to ask questions about them in different ways; and an understanding of when is the most appropriate time to ask these questions. Dispositions are important 'learning outcomes'. They are encouraged rather than taught. To encourage robust dispositions to reason, investigate, and collaborate, children will be immersed in communities where people discuss rules, are fair, explore questions about how things work, and help each other.

(Ministry of Education, 1996: 44)

And in the 2007 redesigned New Zealand school curriculum a similar construct is described as 'key competencies', aligned alongside the strands of curriculum for early childhood (Ministry of Education, 2007b; Carr, 2006; Rychen and Salganik, 2003). This is an interesting development, and will enable, we hope, coherence of learning and learning opportunities across the early childhood, primary and secondary sectors of education.

Resourcefulness and agency as outcomes for education

In thinking about assessment in the multimodal classroom, we have placed human agency and resourcefulness at the centre of what is to be assessed.

(Newfield et al., 2003: 79)

If it is an educational task to assist young people to prepare for a diversity of twenty-first century wildernesses, there is an argument that a major purpose for education is to unlock and open doors to a range of useful resources for learning, and to a range of hitherto unknown 'possible selves' (Marcus and Nurius, 1986). This introduces the constructs of resourcefulness and agency as dispositional outcomes for education.

Resourcefulness

Denise Newfield and colleagues, working in classrooms that use multiple communication and representational resources, describe a 'Tebuwa' cloth, jointly constructed by a group of learners in a High School in South Africa. In this cloth, forms of representation are layered and the process of its making is seen

as a journey across (multi)modes, from the predominantly visual (the maps) to the predominantly linguistic (the contemporary poems), to the three-dimensional (the ethnic dolls), to the multimodal (the praise poems embroidered on the smaller cloths), to the multimodality of the completed artefact.

(Newfield et al., 2003: 75)

They explore the idea of resourcefulness as an overarching category for the development of assessment criteria in a classroom characterized by multiple literacies and multiple ways of knowing.

An example from a New Zealand kindergarten of joint sewing enterprises by three four-year-old children similarly illustrates resourcefulness as a valued outcome. Over several months, the children made an apron, a covered board for Sarah's bedroom (with a sign on it that read 'No shoes allowed in my room'), a motorcycle helmet (out of some black lacy fabric), ambulance jackets and trousers, and bags with printed words and symbols. Resources included a range of interesting fabrics, a sewing machine, fabric dyes, irons, peers as models, consultants and collaborators, one of the children's grandmothers who taught him to sew, and teachers who took an interest, made suggestions, and assisted with the more difficult tasks.

> In our view, Sarah was learning about the 'distributed' nature of persevering with an interest over a long period. She was discovering that learning is distributed or 'stretched over' (Perkins, 1993; Salomon, 1993) peers, teachers, family and material resources, and that to sustain her project, she had to learn to manage this extended network of support.
>
> (Claxton and Carr, 2004: 90–1)

These episodes, an accumulating storyline of resourcefulness, were written up as 'learning stories' in the children's portfolios; the learning was analysed, there were contributions from home as well, and the children revisited the learning at home and at kindergarten.

The High School students in South Africa, and four-year-old Sarah at a kindergarten in New Zealand, were recognizing, orchestrating and constructing affordance networks, with particular intentions in mind.

Agency

Education's task is, at least in part, to suggest 'new directions in which lives may go' as Margaret Donaldson wrote in 1992 (Donaldson, 1992: 259). Bronwyn Davies defines agency as 'a sense of oneself as one who can go beyond the given meanings in any one discourse, and forge something new' (Davies, 1991: 51). She suggests that one way in which this is characterized is through 'imagining not what is, but what might be'. Agency includes developing or adopting particular learning goals and intentions. These are frequently associated with social practices or social communities that appear to be interesting and possible.

In Carol Dweck's book *Mindset: the new psychology of success* (2006), she describes two sets of beliefs about intelligence that are relevant to how we learn. These ideas have been built up from a long period of extensive research (for a summary see Dweck, 1999). The notion of mindset is relevant to the notion of agency. A fixed mindset is one in which one believes that talents and abilities are set in stone – either you have them or you don't, and one cannot imagine that they might change. It is associated with what Dweck calls 'performance' goals. A growth mindset however comes from a belief that talents and abilities are built over time, and can develop in a range of new directions. It is associated with what Dweck calls 'learning' goals. Mindsets and actions associated with agency depend upon the collectives available (children, boys, students, a particular class-room, one's family, etc.), their social practices and the positioning of the person in those practices (Davies, 1990).

Writing about literacy, James Gee says that

> Reading and writing in any domain, whether it be law, biology, literary criticism, rap songs, academic essays, Super Hero comics, or whatever, are not just ways of decoding print, they are also caught up with and in social practices. Literacy in any domain is actually not worth much if one knows nothing about the *social practices* of which the literacy is but a part. And, of course, these social practices involve much more than just an engagement with print … But knowing about a social practice always involves *recognizing* various distinctive ways of acting, interacting, valuing, feeling, knowing, and using various objects and technologies, that constitute the social practice.
>
> (Gee, 2003: 28–9, emphasis in the original)

Gee thus reminds us that learners have not had the same opportunity to learn reading and writing if they have not had the equivalent experience with the social practices associated with reading specific types of text in specific ways. In the same way, learners have not had the same opportunity to practise agency if they have not had the equivalent experience with the social practices where they have been invited to act with agency and responsibility. Pollard and Filer make the same point about strategic action, emphasizing the power structures in the classroom and the way in which children as pupils are positioned within different social practices. Assessment is a key way in which these power structures play out (Filer, 1993).

Combining the work from psychology with Gee's socio-cultural view, we might say that mindsets are embedded in social practices and social communities. Some social practices or social communities are perceived by learners to have fixed boundaries and definitions, set elsewhere, while some social practices or communities are seen as opportunities to explore and redefine boundaries and definitions.

Support for this comes from a research project with four-year-olds. In a study of five activities for which there were ready-to-hand resources available in an early childhood centre I concluded that the activities had become 'homes' or 'dispositional niches' for certain learning dispositions to do with response to challenge and what I called social identities or intents (being a girl/boy, being a technologist or maker of things, being nearly five years old and about to go to school, being a friend). Children appeared to be attracted to those activities that had over time become characterized by orientations that were familiar and comfortable. However, some of the children also responded to opportunities to change their social intents and their orientation towards challenge, often taking up invitations offered by peers (Carr, 2001b, 2002). Although incoming learning dispositions were powerful, the children's early childhood experience also introduced them to new intentions, new directions in which their learning lives may go and invited them to imagine 'possible selves'. For instance, after several episodes of screen printing Danny became aware of the representational qualities of a print and he began to experiment with ways to represent the 'shadow' of his favourite topic, small animals. He was an expert in drawing and in his knowledge of small animals, and this may have made him receptive to resisting the social practice that, in this centre, had grown up around screen printing: performance goals and belonging to the collective of 'being nearly five' children who were allowed to use the screen printer. He appropriated the screen printing process for his favourite interest, being an artist. Linda had none of this background experience, but she used Danny as a model.

> [Danny had] altered the profile of privilege and goal orientation assigned by generations of kindergarteners to screen printing. Linda's goal of being good and her eliciting of approval from adults were themes throughout her work at the construction table; but she, following Danny, became captured by the screen-printing process and began to complete intricate screen prints without assistance or approval.
>
> (Carr, 2001b: 537)

Living in the middle

Resourcefulness and agency are sited in individual-environment transactions. They are about the relationships between the individual and opportunities to learn (Gee, 2003). Another way to look at the environment for the opportunities to learn is to look for the 'mediating means', as, following Vygotsky, James Wertsch calls them. Mediating means are the resources or cultural tools (physical artefacts, symbols, languages, texts, people, as well as routines and social practices) that mediate or assist the learner to get on with the job. Wertsch maintains that just to take the perspective of the individual learner in isolation is not likely to provide an adequate account of human action or agency, and that we should talk about individual(s)-operating-with-mediating-means (Wertsch *et al.*, 1993: 342). He says that this is about 'living in the middle', and comments that 'a focus on mediated action and the cultural tools employed in it makes it possible to "live in the middle" and to address the sociocultural situatedness of action, power and authority' (Wertsch, 1998: 65). 'Living in the middle' (Wertsch says it comes from Holquist, 1994) is a nice phrase, that illustrates the complexity and connect-edness of overarching dispositional categories like resourcefulness and agency, while at the same time it provides us with some considerations for assessment. It reminds us that if we take the perspective of the individual learner in isolation, this is not likely to provide an adequate account. 'Living in the middle' can be a way of describing 'wild' contexts. Learning dispositions will only appear as actions in the classroom or early childhood setting if they have developed over time, are or can be connected to the learners' social intents or goals, and a network of affording resources to exercise them is available. Of course, where desirable learning dispositions are only just developing, the opportunities will need to be more than just available and affording: they may need to invite or actively foster these outcomes in 'sustained shared thinking' (Sylva *et al.*, 2004), routines (Ritchhart, 2002) and assessment practices.

Assessment initiatives

What we would like to avoid is an assessment which in its fixation on the discrete becomes atomized to the extent that the relationships between and beyond are erased.

(Newfield *et al.*, 2003)

What are the implications of this view of learning for formative assessment? There are two reasons why we should consider this question. The first is, that if an aspect of the curriculum that is valued is not assessed in some way, it is likely to disappear from the enacted curriculum (Moss, 1994); assessments in other domains will take its place and the criteria for assessment in those domains will become privileged. The second is that, as research in the Assessment for Learning projects in the UK has illustrated (Black and Wiliam, 1998a, 1998b; Black *et al.*, 2002, 2003), assessment for learning is a key way in which learning is promoted. It can invite and actively foster learning through the use of such strategies as feed-back, self-assessment and revisiting episodes of competence. It illuminates the learning that is valued for learners and their families. It describes learning traject-ories for the interested audiences (teachers, families and learners). It provides a space for conversations about learning between teachers (in those sites where teachers team-teach) and among teachers, learners and families.

In a project for a New Zealand early childhood assessment resource (Ministry of Education, 2005) we have extended the phrase 'noticing, recognizing and responding' as a reference to informal assessment for learning (Cowie, 2000) to analyse assessment for learning as 'noticing, recognizing, responding, recording and revisiting'. Professional development with this resource indicates that as teachers record and revisit the learning, they notice, recognize and respond to children's activities with more understanding. In addition, and relevant to the analysis earlier in this chapter of Sarah's learning, children themselves are beginning to notice, recognize and respond to opportunities for resourcefulness and agency – and to create their own.

Assessments as narratives

Discussions in the United Kingdom on how to develop Assessment for Learning How to Learn (LHTL) (Black *et al.*, 2006) is an example of ongoing work in an area that has some similarities with an interest in the assessment of dispositions to do with acting with agency and being resourceful. Paul Black and colleagues trialled a two-task sequence that focused on assessing pupils' development of 'learning how to learn'. After outlining early attempts to find an assessment instrument, the authors concluded that 'A better alternative might be to develop critical indicators to identify LHTL achievement during normal classroom work, and for teachers to use these in a running record of their pupils' work, over time and across a variety of contexts' (Black *et al.*, 2006: 130). In New Zealand a number of teachers are now using a narrative approach for documentation and assessment, in order not to lose sight of (in the words of the Newfield *et al.* quote at the beginning of this part of the chapter) the key relationships within and beyond: the mediational means. An example of the use of learning stories has already appeared in this chapter: the accumulating evidence for resourcefulness in Sarah's portfolio was built up from a series of learning stories over time and in a range of contexts.

Learning stories are stories of critical episodes of learning, analysed by the writer (usually the teacher, although children and families contribute as well) with learning dispositions and specific criteria in mind. They include a 'What next?' or 'Possible pathways' commentary (Cowie and Carr, 2004 and Carr *et al.*, 2005, include a number of examples). The learning story approach was developed through a research project with teachers looking at the implications for assessment of the early childhood curriculum, Te Whāriki (Carr, 1998a, 1998b, 2001a). The outcomes of the curriculum are expressed in terms of belonging, well-being, exploration, communication and collaboration, and there is an emphasis on learning dispositions as outcomes. These outcomes frame learning in terms of the individual relative to the surrounding world rather than resting on notions of what is 'inside the head of the learner', a perspective that has implications for assessment.

Through the learning story approach the four principles of the curriculum are also applied to assessment. The principles are (Ministry of Education, 1996):

- empowerment (children's self-assessment contributes to their sense of themselves as capable people and competent learners)
- holistic development (working theories and learning dispositions are valued outcomes)
- family and community (families should be part of the assessment)
- relationships (assessment is sited in reciprocal and responsive relationships).

The view of learning embodied by the curriculum also requires a corresponding conception of progress, defined as stories becoming longer, deeper and wider.

Digital technology has enabled the easy use of photographs in these stories, so that children are able to 'read' the stories to families and peers, take their own photographs and dictate the story. At school, children are able to write their own stories. The learning story format provides an opportunity for teachers and learners to refer back to earlier stories and trace a storyline and enables revisiting events of learning and remembering events generally. Here is an example of a learning story where the analysis is addressed to the child.

> It was so good to have the camera handy to catch the magnificent effort of perseverance by Amy today. The first thing that Amy said to me as I approached was, 'I'm getting better and better'. 'What are you doing?' I inquire. 'I'm learning to go over there'. Amy climbs onto the ropes, which I have tied up a day or so earlier. Amy is holding onto these to help her walk across the red ladder. This is not an easy thing to do as the ropes are very loose and this makes balancing somewhat difficult.
>
> I ask you Amy if it used to be hard for you to get across and you tell me that 'Yes, it used to be hard'. We talk together about how with practice it has got easier for you. Amazing!! Now you can go both ways. (Photos of Amy going each way).
>
> ### Short term review/what next
>
> Amy, I really like the way that you are able to see that you are a learner, that sometimes it does take practice to get some things right. Even now as an adult it takes me lots of practice to get some things right.
>
> I would love to see this disposition taken into other areas at kindergarten. Knowing that you can succeed is good to know when you find other things difficult.
>
> (Ministry of Education, 2007a: Book 13)

Research by Katherine Nelson, Robyn Fivush and Catherine Haden has emphasized the contribution of revisiting events and event knowledge to social intent and to making meaning of storylines in young people's lives. 'Children have individual episodic memories from infancy, but it is only in the light of social sharing that both the enduring form of narrative organization, and the perceived value to self and others become apparent' (Nelson, 1997: 111).

> As narrative skills develop, so do skills for representing events in more elaborate, coherent and evaluative forms. Narrating the past is a critical part of representing the past. It is through narrating the personal past that we come to understand and represent the events of our lives in ever more meaningful ways.
>
> (Fivush and Haden, 1997: 195)

Families play a key role in this revisiting, and the research by Pollard and Filer pointed to the influence of families on the children's development of patterns of strategic action. Developing reciprocal relationships between teachers and families, and its value for children's education, is a theme of the research by Norma González, Luis Moll and Cathy Amanti (González *et al.*, 2005, see also Jones, 2006). They write about the value of these relationships in enabling families to feel confident to share with schools the funds of knowledge from home. Parent comments in children's portfolios provide examples of the involvement of families in the early childhood curriculum (and the assessment). Sometimes parent comments will be in the home language, and will be e-mailed, with the story, to family elsewhere. Learning stories have acted as a 'conscription device', a recruitment, into participation for families (Cowie and Carr, 2004: 95). In a story in Nic's portfolio, the teacher has written up a conversation relayed to her by the chef at the childcare centre: Nic asks for fish pie for lunch, and the chef outlines the recipe to him, explaining that she doesn't have enough milk. Nic asks again the next day, and fish pie is put on the menu. There is a comment added by Nic's parents:

> Our kitchen is the focal point of our living area and much time is spent there during our time together as a family. Nic always has an interest in what we are cooking or doing in the kitchen. More recently he has started to get more involved in the goings on in our kitchen, and has helped Mum cook a banana cake and a chocolate cake. He is especially helpful when it is time to eat it!! Maybe we could all make smoked fish pie in our kitchen.
>
> (Ministry of Education, 2007a: Book 12: Wellbeing)

Teachers talk about their assessment journeys

Teachers' journeys with assessment using learning stories have been published in Carr *et al.* (2003), Lee *et al.* (2002) and Hatherly and Sands (2002). Teachers in a number of Ministry-funded action research projects, together with researchers at the University of Waikato, have been exploring aspects of teaching, learning and assessment with learning dispositions or key competencies in mind. In a three-year early childhood Centre of Innovation action research project that focused on the role of ICT in teaching, learning and assessment, learning stories have illustrated the role of the mediational means in children's learning, emphasizing that ICT is just part of this. As an example, Sam took a disposable camera to Samoa when his family returned home there for a visit. When he returned, the teachers scanned the photos and he dictated the accompanying stories to his mother who was, through opportunities at the centre, learning how to use the computer. These stories were added to his portfolio and Sam revisited them with his peers, 'reading' the stories to them. We have used activity theory (see for example Wells and Claxton, 2002; Nardi, 1996) to describe the mediating network and to shape our understanding (Ramsey *et al.*, 2006).

Here are some commentaries from the teachers on the documentation and assessment in this project. The background to the first of these is that four-year-old Mehul, for whom English is not his home language, is unsure about staying without his mother, who tells the teachers that he enjoys helping his older sisters with jobs around the house. So one of the teachers enlists him to help her to laminate some photographs and to use the bookbinder. He watches her photograph the children as they work, and begins to pick up the camera himself to document children's work (for instance when he hears the teacher comment that this is the first time that Sadif has written her name). In the commentary for the project, the teacher says

> This is what Mehul and I did, almost like journalists, working as a team. Mehul then began to take more of an interest in the activities that were available, I think because he had been able to watch and learn about these areas as he documented others. Mehul was now able not only to document his friends' achievements, he was also beginning to document (and recognize) his own … The camera gave Mehul a voice.

The stories in Mehul's portfolio also record his developing use of English language.

> Mehul's use of English developed and you can see in his car story that he was now using full sentences, going from whispering 'camera?' to asking 'Where is the camera, I want to take some pictures.'
>
> (Later) He takes photos of his toy car and is saying: 'This is my car. This is the tyre it has four one two three four. The windows were broken in the shop. I wanted to bring it because I liked to bring and I want to take photos and make a book.'

(Later) He dictates a story to go with a car construction: 'I put here, a sticker, it is the number plate. This is where the driver sits, beside the big part. The nail is the aerial for the radio. The other nail is the seat part for the driver.'

During the project, the teachers comment on the opportunities for agency in this setting:

It's not the teacher that has to instigate or initiate and you sit and watch. We'll do it together.... It's like we're all investigators, and I really notice that with the children. They are confident learners. It's not like they have to wait for the teacher's say-so ... They'll come up and say what do you think about ... or they'll say 'That's a great idea. Do you like that?'

They'll often come looking for us now, won't they, to write their story, because that's what you do. They'll say, 'You need to ... can you come and sit with me 'cos I've got to tell you my story.'

[One of the children] brought an Incredibles book in. She's deeply interested in the Incredibles and Batgirl. And I finished reading it and I said, 'Oh I wish we had a book like this at kindergarten' and then another child pipes up and says, 'We can make one!' and I was a bit blown away because I wouldn't have expected that from her ... And she spent the rest of the morning drawing the characters from it and looking ... and going back and renaming them ... And so for her that was important, to follow the whole process through.

Like if I see something happening I might go and get their portfolio and as I'm working with them I'm flicking through it to see has this happened before? And if it has, how did it happen? And if it hasn't, is there some other connection in your file that's leading to this that's happening now?

Sally Peters and I are currently working with teachers from three schools and two early childhood centres in a Ministry of Education funded Teaching and Learning Research Initiative project entitled Key Learning Competencies across Place and Time. Teachers in two of the schools chose to explore Learning Stories as a way of documenting and assessing learning dispositions and key competencies. Here are teacher comments from Nikki in Working Paper 5.

Being a progressive school, we were interested in finding a way of assessing which reflected our philosophy. Learning Stories appeared to be a natural fit as this approach allowed us to document real learning as it occurred.

I feel comfortable using the Key Competencies with Learning Stories as both enable me to capture learning as it occurs naturally. The Key Competencies lead beyond the learning of discrete skills and towards the bigger picture, honouring the values, attitudes and dispositions that help us become empowered learners in and out of school.

(O'Connor, 2006: 3)

During the third year of the project Nikki has begun to ask the children for their criteria, in their own words: 'Giving it a go' or 'Trying something new' are examples. She has been exploring ways to develop an electronic learning story database, to enable storylines across time and place to be developed and shared with children and families. Here are teacher comments from Yvonne in Working Paper 4.

> When I shared the news of the Curriculum review and my understanding of the draft Key Competencies with my colleagues, the reaction of colleagues was not positive, with comments of 'What next!' and 'How are we going to fit that in?' Their reaction was hardly surprising ... I decided to explore how the draft key Competencies could be integrated into the daily programme, and assessed, without creating extra workload for teachers already struggling with an overcrowded curriculum. Literacy and numeracy are the main thrusts in the junior classes so I decided to start with these curriculum areas, hence the research question: How can the draft Key Competencies be integrated into literacy and numeracy? My original Learning Story format had space to analyse Key Competency learning only. My first step was to modify the format to include space to analyse the learning in both areas, Key Competencies and the Learning Areas.

> The literacy stories show children developing oral and written skills at the same time as aspects of the Key Competencies. Likewise the maths stories highlight children developing the Key Competencies as well as number strategy and knowledge.

(Smith *et al.*, 2006: 3, 4)

Yvonne writes stories for individuals, small groups and the whole class. In one of her Maths stories, when Luke called out a (correct) answer to a subtraction problem, Yvonne writes: '"How do you know?" I asked. He proceeded to explain to the other children, using his counters to demonstrate. He was very excited about this and was keen to teach others his discovery.' The analysis of the learning for Key Competencies included commentary on Luke's involvement in the activity and his teaching; the analysis for the Learning Areas summarized his maths strategies.

Conclusion

This chapter has argued for a consideration of learning dispositions, under various names, as outcomes for education: if they include attunement to resource networks and connections to social intents and social practices, then they can provide a more adequate account of learning. They are useful 'in the wild' where occasions and situations may be vaguely marked and not well defined, and for this reason too they have the potential to be future-focused, to set some lifelong learning pathways in train. But these outcomes, learning dispositions and key competencies for instance, are 'fuzzy'. Their shape is indistinct, their boundaries unclear and their scope is uncertain. Resourcefulness and agency were discussed as examples of overarching categories of learning disposition. Resourcefulness is especially connected to the material and human resources available. Agency appears to be especially connected to the interests, social practices and 'possible selves' that are available. In a number of projects in New Zealand early years settings, teachers have been researching ways to assess dispositional aspects of learning that include the children's interests and the affording context. They are using learning stories to do this, in order keep the relationships documented as well as the knowledge and the skill, and to prepare assessments that speak to families.

Elliot Eisner, an American writer about teaching and learning who describes teaching as an art rather than a science, has commented that teachers are the people who can best recognize the value of students' questions, their degree of engagement, the quality of their relationships and the level of imagination they have displayed. He added:

> As researchers, we need to design practices in which teachers pay systematic attention to such features and prepare short narratives that would provide a much more replete picture of assessment than a B+ or an 82 on a standardized achievement test.

> (Eisner, 2000: 351)

This chapter has described some of the ways that teachers, in collaboration with researchers and professional development providers, are beginning to do this. It is a work in progress. It seems important however, that the opportunities to learn are in some way included in the documentation: for an adequate account of learning as well as for the reason that assessment itself is an opportunity to foster resourcefulness and agency.

Points for reflection

1. To what extent do your current assessment practices promote resourcefulness and agency? How could they be developed to do so?
2. What insights are triggered for you by thinking of assessment for learning as 'noticing, recognizing, responding, recording and revisiting'?
3. What do you see as the benefits of a learning story approach to assessment and recording? What steps could you take towards developing a culture of learning stories?

Acknowledgements

The author acknowledges the New Zealand Ministry of Education for funding for three projects that contributed to the ideas in this chapter: the Early Childhood Learning and Assessment Project, directed by the author and Wendy Lee, which developed a resource for early childhood teachers, Kei tua o te pae. Assessment for Learning: early childhood exemplars, the Roskill South Kindergarten Centre of Innovation project, and the Teaching and Learning Research Initiative project Key Learning Competencies over Place and Time. The views expressed here are the author's and not necessarily those of the Ministry of Education. Thank you also to my co-researchers and to the professional development providers, the teachers, the children and the families in these projects for their assistance, their commentaries and their stories.

Further reading

The following provide sources of examples and further ideas on this topic:

Carr, M. (2001) *Assessment in Early Childhood Settings: learning stories*, London: Paul Chapman.

Cowie, B. and Carr, M. (2004) 'The consequences of socio-cultural assessment', in A. Anning, J. Cullen and M. Fleer (eds) *Early Childhood Education: society and culture*, London: Sage.

Ministry of Education (2005) *Kei tua o te pae. Assessment for Learning: early childhood exemplars* Books 1–9, Wellington: Learning Media.

—— (2007) *Kei tua o te pae. Assessment for Learning: early childhood exemplars* Books 10–15, Wellington: Learning Media.

References

Barab, S.A. and Roth, W-M. (2006) 'Curriculum-based ecosystems: supporting knowing from an ecological perspective', *Educational Researcher* 35: 3–13.

Bereiter, C. (1995) 'A dispositional view of transfer', in A. McKeough, J.L. Lupart and A. Marini (eds) *Teaching for Transfer: fostering generalization in learning*, Mahwah, NJ: Lawrence Erlbaum.

Black, P. and Wiliam, D. (1998a) 'Assessment and classroom learning', *Assessment in Education*, 5: 7–74.

—— (1998b) *Inside the Black Box: raising standards through classroom assessment*, London: School of Education, King's College.

Black, P., Harrison, C., Lee, C., Marshall, B. and Wiliam, D. (2002) *Working Inside the Black Box*, London: School of Education, King's College.

—— (2003) *Assessment for Learning: putting it into practice*, Maidenhead: Open University Press.

Black, P., McCormick, R., James, M. and Pedder, D. (2006) 'Learning how to learn and assessment for learning: a theoretical enquiry', *Research Papers in Education*, 21: 119–32.

Bransford, J.D. and Schwartz, D.L. (1999) 'Re-thinking transfer: a simple proposal with multiple implications', *Review of Research in Education*, 24: 61–100.

Carr, M. (1998a) *Assessing Children's Experiences in Early Childhood. Final report to the Ministry of Education*, Wellington: Ministry of Education.

—— (1998b) *Assessing Children's Learning in Early Childhood Settings*. A professional development programme for discussion and reflection. Three videos and a support booklet, Wellington: NZCER.

—— (2001a) *Assessment in Early Childhood Settings: learning stories*, London: Paul Chapman.

—— (2001b) 'A sociocultural approach to learning orientation in an early childhood setting', *Qualitative Studies in Education*, 14: 525–42.

—— (2002) 'Emerging learning narratives: a perspective from early childhood education', in G. Wells and G. Claxton (eds) *Learning for Life in the 21st Century: sociocultural perspectives on the future of education*, Oxford: Blackwell.

—— (2006) 'Learning dispositions and key competencies: a new continuity of curriculum across the sectors?', *set*, 2: 23–7.

Carr, M., Hatherly, A., Lee, W. and Ramsey, K. (2003) 'Te Whāriki and assessment: a case study of teacher change', in J. Nuttall (ed.) *Weaving Te Whāriki: Aotearoa New Zealand's early childhood curriculum document in theory and practice*, Wellington: NZCER.

Carr, M., Lee, W. and Jones, C. (2005) 'Beyond listening: can assessment play a part?' in A. Clark, A.T. Kjørholt and P. Moss (eds) *Beyond Listening: children's perspectives on early childhood services*, Bristol: Policy Press.

Claxton, G. and Carr, M. (2004) A framework for teaching learning: the dynamics of disposition, *Early Years*, 24: 87–97.

Claxton, G.L. (2002) *Building Learning Power: helping young people to become better learners*, Bristol: TLO Ltd.

Costa A.L. and Kallick, B. (2000) (eds) *Assessing and Reporting on Habits of Mind*, Alexandria, VA: Association for Supervision and Curriculum Development.

Cowie, B. (2000) 'Formative assessment in science classrooms', unpublished thesis submitted in fulfilment for the degree of PhD, University of Waikato, Hamilton.

Cowie, B. and Carr, M. (2004) 'The consequences of socio-cultural assessment', in A. Anning, J. Cullen and M. Fleer (eds) *Early Childhood Education: society and culture*, London: Sage.

Cunha, F., Heckman, J.J., Lochner, L. and Masterov, D. (2005) 'Interpreting the evidence on life cycle skill formation', *British Educational Research Journal*, 30: 713–30.

Davies, B. (1990) 'Agency as a form of discursive practice. A classroom scene observed', *British Journal of Sociology of Education*, 11: 341–61.

—— (1991) 'The concept of agency: a feminist poststructuralist analysis', *Social Analysis*, 30: 42–53.

Donaldson, M. (1992) *Human Minds: an exploration*, London: Penguin.

Dweck, C.S. (1999) *Self-Theories: their role in motivation, personality, and development*, Philadelphia, PA: Psychology Press.

—— (2006) *Mindset: the new psychology of success*, New York: Random House.

Eisner, E. (2000) 'Those who ignore the past . . .: 12 'easy' lessons for the next millennium', *Journal of Curriculum Studies*, 32: 343–57.

Filer, A. (1993) 'The assessment of classroom language: challenging the rhetoric "objectivity"', *International Studies in Sociology of Education*, 5: 183–212.

Filer, A. with Pollard, A. (2000) *The Social World of Children's Learning: case studies of pupils from four to seven*, London: Cassell.

Fivush, R. and Haden, C.A. (1997) 'Narrating and representing experience: preschoolers' developing autobiographical accounts', in P.W. Van den Broek, P.J. Bauer and T. Bourg (eds) *Developmental Spans in Event Comprehension and Representation: bridging fictional and actual events*, Mahwah, NJ: Lawrence Erlbaum.

Gee, J.P. (2003) 'Opportunity to learn: a language-based perspective on assessment', *Assessment in Education*, 10: 27–46.

Gonzalez, N., Moll, L.C. and Amanti, C. (2005) *Funds of Knowledge: theorizing practices in households, communities and classrooms*, Mahwah, NJ: Lawrence Erlbaum.

Greeno, J.G., Collins, A.M. and Resnick, L.B. (1996) 'Cognition and learning', in D.C. Berliner and R.C. Calfee (eds) *Handbook of Educational Psychology*, New York: Simon and Schuster Macmillan, and London: Prentice Hall.

Hatherly, A. and Sands, L. (2002) 'So what is different about learning stories? The first years', *Nga Tau Tuatahi*, 4: 8–13.

Holquist, M. (1994) 'The reterritorialization of the enthymeme', Paper presented at the International Conference on Vygotsky and the Human Sciences, Moscow, September.

Jones, C. (2006) 'Continuity of learning: adding funds of knowledge from the home environment', *set*, 2: 28–31.

Lee, W., Hatherly, A. and Ramsey, K. (2002) 'Using ICT to document children's learning', *Early Childhood Folio*, 6: 10–16.

Marcus, H. and Nurius, P. (1986) 'Possible Selves', *American Psychologist*, September: 954–69.

Ministry of Education (1996) *Te Whāriki. He Whariki Mātauranga mö ngä Mokopuna o Aotearoa: early childhood curriculum*, Wellington: Learning Media.

—— (2005) *Kei tua o te pae. Assessment for learning: early childhood exemplars* Books 1–9, Wellington: Learning Media.

—— (2007a) *Kei tua o te pae. Assessment for Learning: early childhood exemplars* Books 10–15. Wellington: Learning Media.

—— (2007b) *The New Zealand Curriculum for English-medium Teaching and learning in Years 1–13*, Wellington: Learning Media.

Moss, P.A. (1994) 'Can there be validity without reliability?' *Educational Researcher*, March, 5–12.

Nardi, B.A. (ed.) (1996) *Context and Consciousness: activity theory and human-computer interaction*. Cambridge, MA: The MIT Press.

Nelson, K. (1997) 'Cognitive change as collaborative construction', in E. Amsel and K.A. Renninger (eds) *Change and Development: issues of theory, method and application*, Mahwah, NJ: Lawrence Erlbaum.

Newfield, D., Andrew, D., Stein, P. and Maungedzo, R. (2003) 'No number can describe how good it was: assessment issues in the multimodal classroom', *Assessment in Education*, 10: 61–81.

O'Connor, N. (2006) 'Establishing a key competencies and learning story database', Working Paper 5. Key learning competencies across place and time. Hamilton: University of Waikato Wilf Malcolm Institute of Educational Research.

Perkins, D. (2000) 'Schools need to pay more attention to "intelligence in the wild"', *Harvard Education Newsletter* May/June: 7–8.

Perkins, D., Tishman, S., Ritchhart, R., Donis, K. and Andrade, A. (2000) 'Intelligence in the wild: a dispositional view of intellectual traits', *Educational Psychology Review*, 12: 269–93.

Perkins, D. (1993) 'Person-plus: a distributed view of thinking and learning', in G. Salomon (ed.) *Distributed Cognitions: psychological and educational considerations*, Cambridge: Cambridge University Press.

Perkins, D., Jay, E. and Tishman, S. (1993) 'Beyond abilities: a dispositional theory of thinking', *Merrill-Palmer Quarterly*, 39: 1–21.

Peters, S. (2004) 'Crossing the border: an interpretive study of children making the transition to school', unpublished thesis submitted in fulfilment for the degree of PhD, University of Waikato, Hamilton.

Pollard, A. and Filer, A. (1999) *The Social World of Pupil Career*, London: Cassell.

—— (1996) *The Social World of Children's Learning: case studies of pupils from four to seven*, London: Cassell.

Ramsey, K., Breen, J., Sturm, J., Lee, W. and Carr, M. (2006) *Strengthening Learning and Teaching using ICT*, Final report to the Ministry of Education on a Centre of Innovation project, Hamilton: University of Waikato Wilf Malcolm Institute of Educational Research.

Ritchhart, R. (2002) *Intellectual Character: what it is, why it matters, and how to get it*, San Francisco: Jossey-Bass.

Rychen, D.S. and Salganik, L.H. (2003) (eds) *Key Competencies for a Successful Life and a Well-Functioning Society*, Göttingen: Hogrefe and Huber.

Salomon, G. (1993) *Distributed Cognitions: psychological and educational considerations*, Cambridge: Cambridge University Press.

Sizer, T.R. (1992) *Horace's School: redesigning the American high school*, Boston: Houghton Mifflin.

Smith, Y. with Molloy, S. and Davis, K. (2006) 'The integration of key competencies with literacy and numeracy', Working Paper 4. Key Learning Competencies across Place and Time. Hamilton: University of Waikato Wilf Malcolm Institute of Educational Research.

Sylva, K., Melhuish, E., Sammons, P., Siraj-Blatchford, I. and Taggert, B. (2004) 'The final report: effective preschool education', Researching Effective Pedagogy in the Early Years Technical Paper 12. London: Institute of Education University of London.

Tuomi-Gröhn, T. and Engeström, Y. (2003) 'Conceptualizing transfer: from standard notions to developmental perspectives', in Tuomi-Gröhn, T., Engeström, Y. and Young, M. (eds) *Between School and Work: new perspectives on transfer and boundary-crossing*, London: Pergamon.

Tuomi-Gröhn, T., Engeström, Y. and Young, M. (eds) (2003) *Between School and Work: new perspectives on transfer and boundary-crossing*, London: Pergamon.

Wells, G. (2002) 'Enquiry as an orientation for learning, teaching and teacher education', in G. Wells and G. Claxton (eds) *Learning for Life in the 21st Century*, Oxford, Blackwell.

Wells, G. and Claxton, G. (eds) (2002) *Learning for Life in the 21st Century*, Oxford: Blackwell.

Wertsch, J.V. (1998) *Mind as Action*, New York: Oxford University Press.

Wertsch, J.V., Tulviste, P. and Hagstrom, F. (1993) 'A sociocultural approach to agency', in E.A. Forman, N. Minick and C.A. Stone (eds) *Contexts for Learning: sociocultural dynamics in children's development*, New York: Oxford University Press.

PART II

Assessment for learning

Feedback

The central process in assessment for learning

Sue Swaffield

Feedback is one of the most powerful influences on learning and achievement, but this impact can be either positive or negative.

(Hattie and Timperley, 2007: 81)

Introduction

This straightforward statement by John Hattie and Helen Timperley is hugely important, and sets the agenda for this chapter. Feedback is part of everyday life and takes many forms, for example a comment from a family member, friend or colleague, the reading on the bathroom scales or the response to a job application. A few moments' reflection will bring to mind the variety of feelings generated by receiving feedback, and its effects and consequences. In education feedback is generally considered 'a good thing', although this is not necessarily the case. Feedback is powerful, but since its effects can be for good or ill we need to consider it carefully, strive to understand its complexities and nuances, and seek to ensure that feedback supports rather than frustrates our educational aims.

Feedback takes many forms, oral and written, and includes marking. This chapter examines feedback in the classroom and concentrates on its relationship with pupils' learning, although of course feedback can also be about other things, for example behaviour or teaching. The chapter draws on literature and relates the issues to those raised in other chapters in this volume. It starts with an overview of feedback, its relationship to assessment for learning (AfL) and other key concepts, before discussing the types and effects of feedback. The processes of giving and acting on feedback are then considered, followed by reflection on issues such as culture and context.

The term feedback has its origins in regulatory mechanisms, where part of the 'output' of a system is returned or fed back to it in a way that affects its performance, keeping it 'on track'. This process of readjustment has close parallels with teachers using feedback to guide teaching and learning on a course most likely to reach a predetermined goal. However, learning can be open-ended with novel or surprising outcomes, and here feedback has a different role, perhaps suggesting a general direction or the exploration of uncharted routes. Creativity has perhaps traditionally been associated with the arts, but originality and innovation are very important in all areas of the curriculum. The possible tension between feedback related to preconceived goals as opposed to 'fuzzy outcomes' (see Margaret Carr's chapter) or a 'horizon of possibilities' (see Mary James' chapter) is a theme running throughout this chapter.

The idea of future performance being affected by information about previous performance is central to learning. It is often expressed in terms of closing the gap between current and desired performance, and in defining feedback both Ramaprasad (1983) and Sadler (1989) stress that the information has to be *used* to alter the gap, otherwise it is not feedback. This resonates with the Assessment Reform Group's (ARG) definition of assessment for learning as 'the process of seeking and interpreting evidence for use by learners and their teachers to decide where the learners are in their learning, where they need to go and how best to get there' (ARG, 2002a).

So feedback is an integral part of assessment for learning, and is one of the central strands of formative assessment (ARG 1999, 2002a; Black and Wiliam, 1998a). Below are listed the ten principles underpinning assessment for learning (ARG, 2002a), many of which relate directly to feedback.

Assessment for learning:

- is part of effective planning
- focuses on how pupils learn
- is central to classroom practice
- is a key professional skill
- is sensitive and constructive
- fosters motivation
- promotes understanding of goals and criteria
- helps learners know how to improve
- develops the capacity for self (and peer) assessment
- recognizes all educational achievement.

These principles play out differently in different contexts, depending for example on whether the learning goals are predetermined or open-ended, but remain a very useful guide and checklist for practice. The 'Learning How to Learn' project (James *et al.*, 2007) built on previous AfL development and research work, and identified two key features of classroom practice – 'making learning explicit' and 'promoting learning autonomy'. These emphasize the importance of sharing and making visible learning aims, processes and outcomes, and of pupils taking responsibility for and directing their own learning. Here again feedback is integral to these processes.

Feedback, values, agency and theories of learning

There are many strong links between feedback and the ideas discussed in the chapters in the first part of this volume. Mary-Jane Drummond argues that there is a close relationship between what we value and what we choose to assess. By extension what we choose to give feedback on, itself a subset of everything that we assess, conveys strong messages about what we value, messages that are clearly interpreted by pupils. Margaret Carr argues that assessment is an opportunity to foster resourcefulness and agency, and certainly the prompts and suggestions that we offer to students and the nature of the feedback we give can encourage autonomous approaches to learning. Conversely, if we create the impression through our feedback that there is only one way of achieving something, that teachers know best and will tell children what to do, agency and resourcefulness will be stifled.

In her chapter Mary James sets out three differing views of learning and examines their implications for assessment (see also James, 2006). Susan Askew and Caroline Lodge have undertaken a similar analysis in relation to models of learning and feedback (Askew and Lodge, 2000). These and other authors (for example Bredo, 1997; Watkins, 2003; Pollard *et al.*, 2005) each identify three ways of thinking about learning, even though they use different terms and emphasize different points.

The most established of the three theories of learning is described by Chris Watkins as 'learning is being taught' (Watkins, 2003). Askew and Lodge refer to something similar in describing learning and teaching in terms of reception and transmission, emphasizing the respective roles of pupil and teacher. The model rests on the assumption that there is a body of knowledge that the teacher possesses, and it is his/her job to pass this on to students, while their job is to absorb, retain and use it. Learning is something that pupils do as individuals, and the best learners (the 'most able') quickly acquire a stock of knowledge. With this characterization of learning, feedback tends to focus on how much the pupil has learned, on misconceptions and mistakes, and notions of right and wrong. Askew and Lodge term feedback given by teacher to learner in this model as a gift, drawing attention to the one-way nature of the communication and the dependency that it fosters. Feedback that expresses the teacher's pleasure or satisfaction is akin to a reward reinforcing desired behaviour, underlining the close association of this model of learning with behaviourism. A gift carries assumptions that the recipient is pleased to receive it, and that it will be of benefit. However, much feedback associated with the view that 'learning is being taught' is neither pleasurable nor necessarily appreciated, while its positive influence on learning is questionable.

A constructivist model of learning, described by Watkins (2003) as 'learning as individual sense-making', takes the emphasis away from teachers' efforts to transmit knowledge as a discrete entity, towards assisting learners to construct meaning by relating new experiences to established understandings. In this model learners are viewed as actively developing thinking rather than passively receiving knowledge. New learning is highly dependent on prior learning, and so teachers must explore pupils' current understanding in order to support further development. Feedback is then used by teachers to check out their perceptions, and to offer pupils points for reflection. So rather than a single, one-way communication, feedback becomes more of a discussion, termed by Askew and Lodge (2000) as 'ping-pong'. However, it can too easily become a rather one-sided game, as power still resides with the teacher who is always the one to initiate play and to serve.

In the constructivist model of learning, as with the receptive-transmission model, learning is an individual process, which contrasts with the third view of learning – the co-constructivist or socio-cultural model. The essence of this third perspective is that learning comes about through interacting with others in meaningful contexts. Whilst not commonly found in classrooms, genuine group projects and problem-solving activities exemplify this way of working. Pupils learn as much from each other as from the teacher, whose role is to facilitate authentic activities and to scaffold learning. Feedback is part of ongoing dialogue, which is as likely to be initiated by pupils as by the teacher, and to which pupils contribute their expertise so that everyone learns, teacher included. The distinctions between learners and teachers are blurred, and reciprocal feedback is integrated into learning so that it resembles developing loops (Askew and Lodge, 2000). This term calls to mind the single and double loop learning described by Peter Senge (1992), where double loop learning involves standing outside the process of 'plan–implement–evaluate' to reflect upon the process and the goals themselves.

Types of feedback

The three models of feedback discussed above are lenses through which the complexity of feedback has begun to be revealed. One structure for exploring this complexity further is Rudyard Kipling's 'faithful companions' – the questions why, who, what, when and how.

Why

As noted above, Ramaprasad (1983) and Sadler (1989) understand feedback as a process for closing the gap between current and desired performance, but other authors take a rather broader view, perceiving feedback as serving a diversity of purposes. A basic but important distinction among possible purposes lies in the formative and summative aims of assessment (an issue explored in more depth in Wynne Harlen's chapter in this volume). Formative feedback is concerned with contributing to future development and tends to be more process orientated, whereas feedback related to summative purposes has a more evaluative focus. As Mary James observes, there can be 'a tension between developmental and accountability purposes' of feedback (James, 1998: 96). Harry Torrance and John Pryor propose a conceptual framework composed of two (not necessarily mutually exclusive) approaches to classroom assessment, which they term convergent and divergent (Torrance and Pryor, 1998), broadly paralleling summative and formative purposes of assessment. The aim of convergent assessment is 'to discover *whether* the learner knows, understands or can do a predetermined thing' while divergent assessment 'aims to discover *what* the learner knows, understands or can do' (italics in original) (Torrance and Pryor, 1998: 153). Feedback of convergent assessment tends towards the judgemental, whereas with divergent assessment the emphasis is on descriptive feedback.

Pat Tunstall and Caroline Gipps suggest a typology of assessment and feedback with four elements – evaluative (expressing approval/disapproval and encouraging effort), descriptive specifying attainment (pointing out successes), descriptive specifying improvement (identifying mistakes and how work can be improved) and constructing (more of a conversation, encouraging self-assessment) (Tunstall and Gipps, 1996; Gipps, 1996). As will be explored in more detail later in the chapter, feedback that supports assessment for learning often consists of the second and third types specifying success and offering a specific focus for improvement. 'Constructing achievement' feedback differs from the other three forms in that the learner and the teacher together identify and discuss achievement and the way forward.

Who

Who is involved with feedback? Who creates it? Who is it for? The traditional view is of feedback being given by the teacher to the student, but students can also give feedback to teachers, and a number of other people can be involved. Pupils can give feedback to each other, as in peer assessment, or to themselves through self-assessment (an area explored in this volume by Lorna Earl and Steven Katz). Parents may be givers, receivers or co-constructors. Additional audiences for written feedback include other teachers and learning assistants, school leaders and inspectors. Learners may even be provided with feedback by technology rather than by a person (see Martin Ripley's chapter). While deprived of the human touch, well-calibrated feedback by learning programmes can be more encouraging and less threatening than that offered by teachers with whom prior history may contaminate the interaction.

What

Another way of looking at feedback is to consider its focus. What is it about? As has already been noted, we convey messages about what we value through the things we choose to comment on, and so we should always be mindful of the subjects of assessment and feedback. Since feedback is conceived of as supporting improvement, feedback should be about whatever it is we are trying to improve. That sounds straightforward, but Paul Black and Dylan Wiliam's review of formative assessment reported 'a tendency to emphasize quantity and presentation of work and to neglect its quality in relation to learning' (Black and Wiliam, 1998b: 6).

John Hattie and Helen Timperley (2007) propose a model of feedback that includes three major questions that feedback must answer, as well as four levels at which the questions should be asked. The questions relate both to desired and current performance and how to close the gap: Where am I going? (goals) How am I going? (progress) and Where to next? (actions to take). Hattie and Timperley claim that:

> How effectively answers to these questions serve to reduce the gap is partly dependent on the level at which the feedback operates. These include the level of performance task, the level of process of understanding how to do a task, the regulatory or metacognitive process level, and/or the self or personal level (unrelated to the specifics of the task).
>
> (Hattie and Timperley, 2007: 86)

Their argument that feedback about the self as a person is the least effective concurs with other findings that feedback should be about the task not the learner (ARG, 2002b).

Another aspect of the 'what' of feedback is the basis for comparison – criteria or models of quality, previous performance, or other students. Of these three referencing systems it is the later normative approach that is most entrenched and yet often has negative consequences. (The chapter by Pete Dudley and Sue Swaffield discusses norm, criterion and ipsative referencing in more detail.)

When

Feedback that is integrated with teaching and learning of necessity takes place during and throughout the period of time, as opposed to feedback that is discrete and is not received until some time after the activity to which it refers. In the case of some examinations the delay can be weeks or even months, by which time students have almost certainly moved on (or regressed) in their learning, and most probably have forgotten the detail, so that the feedback can have only a very limited improvement function. Errors or misconceptions may have become habitual and so be much more difficult to redress. By contrast, simultaneous feedback has the potential to be precisely focused and to be acted on immediately, so that improvements can be made and recognized instantly. However, continuous feedback may be distracting and encourage dependency, so achieving the balance in timescales between these two ends of the spectrum is generally both practical and appropriate.

How

The how of feedback is closely related to the when, with oral feedback generally used when it is completely integrated with teaching and learning, although technology also makes instant feedback possible. Written feedback is the form most often used when it is given after the event, and is often necessitated by the teacher being unable to attend to everyone at once and therefore taking work away to mark later. Whether feedback is oral or written the detail can vary enormously, for example from a quick acknowledgement, grade or score, to a meticulous in-depth commentary. We also give feedback in other ways, for example by assigning children to particular groups, and through intonation, body language, and other non-verbal strategies (Hargreaves *et al.*, 2000). Such things send extremely strong messages even if they are subconscious or unplanned.

Effects of feedback

Researchers have examined the effects of feedback (interpreted broadly) both qualitatively and quantitatively. A few examples illuminate key points.

Many studies and meta-analyses have quantified effect sizes, which is a way of measuring gains in scores. One of the most extensive studies was 'a synthesis of over 500 meta-analyses, involving 450,000 effect sizes from 180,000 studies, representing approximately 20 to 30 million students' (Hattie and Timperley, 2007: 82). This study revealed an average effect size of 0.4, a figure also arrived at by Black and Wiliam (1998b), and Kluger and DeNisi (1996) who analysed 131 reports involving over 12,652 participants and 607 effect sizes. However, the most important point is that 0.4 is the *average* effect size, which masks great variation. Kluger and DeNisi found that 40 per cent of the effects were negative. So it is not the presence or absence of feedback that makes a difference, but its nature and quality. With these arresting findings, researchers have attempted to unravel the detail and discover what it is that actually makes feedback effective.

One perspective suggests that this may be a fruitless quest, since people respond quite differently to what may appear on the surface to be the same feedback. It seems to depend on the recipient, and their relationship with the feedback provider. Do I trust this person and believe that they have my best interests at heart? Or do I suspect that the feedback reflects another less benevolent agenda? Alternatively, interpretations of feedback may be coloured by self-image and notions of ability: 'I am just no good at art, and nothing will ever alter that.' Thoughts such as these may not be conscious, but they can have a profound influence, and indicate the complex interplay of assessment with motivation and self-esteem. Carol Dweck's research (Dweck, 1999, 2006) on the theories we hold about ourselves and how these are influenced by the feedback we receive, our views about the nature of 'ability' and the different factors to which we attribute success, is very relevant here.

Whilst acknowledging the undoubted influence of the individual, much detailed work has been done to identify the characteristics of more and less effective feedback. For example, Kluger and DeNisi (1996) separated the effects of different types of feedback and concluded (among other things) that feedback is more effective when it concentrates on success rather than failure, and that praise is ineffective. But even specific forms of feedback are not universally effective, with differential effects found for high and low attainers (Black and Wiliam, 1998a).

These examples of large-scale statistical studies into the effects of feedback provide helpful insights as well as pointing to some of the complexities. Two researchers in Germany set up a study to look at motivational and cognitive processes involved in feedback influencing learning. Their findings surprised them: it was not just the feedback that had an effect, but the *expectation* of receiving it (Vollmeyer and Rheinberg, 2005). Students who anticipated feedback used better learning strategies than those who did not, which has implications for what we tell pupils in advance about how their work will be assessed.

A rich and fascinating qualitative study by Harry Torrance and John Pryor revealed the complex minutiae of formative assessment. The research involved detailed analysis of classroom assessment practice using observation, transcripts of classroom interactions and interviews. The significance of their work is illustrated by the following quotation:

> Once again we are faced with two incidents that at first sight may seem rather insignificant, yet they constitute exactly the sort of myriad routine interactions which lay down the 'sediment' of student identity and self-esteem with respect to the process of schooling. And below the surface, complex issues are being played out.
>
> (Torrance and Pryor, 1998: 99)

The data and accompanying commentary clearly demonstrated that assessment, in which feedback is central, has both positive and negative impact on pupils' learning, and the effects are due to the interplay of social, psychological and cognitive issues. In their conclusion the authors state that teaching, learning and assessment is social interaction between teachers and their pupils '... not a set of procedures that can be unilaterally invoked by teachers' (Torrance and Pryor, 1998: 168).

The feedback process

If we accept that assessment is not a 'set of procedures' but rather a pedagogic process in which social interaction is a key determinant, we can identify some implications and pointers for practice. Since the following chapter in this volume by Jeremy Hodgen and Mary Webb focuses on questioning and dialogue, which includes oral feedback, here I concentrate on guidance about feedback in general and written feedback in particular.

There is considerable agreement among assessment researchers (for example: Black and Wiliam, 1998a, b; Clarke, 2003, 2005a, b; Kluger and DeNisi, 1996; James, 1998; Sadler, 1989) about the key elements of feedback. They all relate feedback to the three aspects of 'closing the gap', embedded in the ARG (2002a) definition of assessment for learning: 'where learners are, where they need to go, and how best to get there'. In summary, feedback should:

- focus on student learning
- focus on the task rather than the learner
- focus on process rather than product
- focus on progress
- focus on particular qualities of the work
- advise how to improve
- encourage the student to think
- require action that is challenging yet achievable
- be specific
- avoid comparison with others
- be understandable to the student.

Clear flexible intentions

Focusing feedback and being specific about where pupils are in their learning is much easier when teachers are clear about learning intentions. National curriculum and national strategy materials have proved helpful in planning and specifying learning intentions. Sharing the learning objective, returning to it in plenary and marking work against it have become routine procedures in many classrooms.

This has undoubtedly helped focus learning and feedback, although we need to be alert to the dangers of such practice becoming ritualized and procedural (Marshall and Drummond, 2006). Shirley Clarke's work with teachers, examining the nature of learning intentions, advises a separation of the intention from the context and the activity (Clarke, 2003). For example, the teacher may have decided to use the context of making jelly for the learning intention 'to be able to write instructions', and separating the two helps keep the focus on the features of writing instructions rather than getting distracted by irrelevant details of making jelly such as the flavour or mould shape. This practice, together with explicit success criteria (best devised with the children) has really helped teachers to focus feedback appropriately.

However, although clear specific learning intentions can be helpful in supporting some forms of learning, they can also be limiting. One wonders how Tom whom we met in Mary-Jane Drummond's chapter, or the various children whose stories we read in Margaret Carr's chapter, would fare in a school dominated by a set sequence of specific learning objectives. Making a distinction here between intentions and objectives is deliberate: as Elliot Eisner points out, intentions are not fixed but are 'flexible purposing' (Eisner, 2002: 52), a phrase borrowed from John Dewey that 'pertains to the improvisational side of intelligence as it is employed in the arts' (Eisner, 2002: 77). The point is that we need different kinds of objectives for different kinds of learning, for example expressive creative activities or problem-solving situations, reminding us again that it is not always possible or appropriate to pre-specify learning. Rather than a predetermined fixed point it may be better to think in terms of a horizon of possibilities.

Written feedback

So how can the principles and ideas proposed here be put into practice when providing written feedback? Written feedback, also known as marking, has in the past sometimes been little more than 'flick and tick' – flicking through the students' books to check that they have done the work, with occasional ticks as acknowledgement and to provide evidence that the teacher has 'marked' the books. In contrast, students' work was often covered in marks (traditionally in red pen) as a result of teachers identifying every error, particularly in presentational aspects such as spelling and punctuation. Often these teachers too were conscious of the possibility of other eyes (belonging to parents, the headteacher or inspectors) scrutinizing their marking, and were wary of 'missing' any mistakes.

Both 'flick and tick' and 'cover everything in red' marking were often accompanied by a numerical mark or grade and a comment at the end of the work. The practice of giving marks and comments has come under particular scrutiny as the result of a study by Ruth Butler. Her research (Butler, 1988) featured in the

Black and Wiliam's review (1998a) and has since been widely quoted and publicized. In controlled experimental conditions Butler looked at the effects on learning and motivation of providing three types of feedback – grades, grades and comments, and comments only. She found that neither grades alone nor grades and comments resulted in learning improvements, a finding that has led to the adoption of 'comment only' marking policies.

The beneficial effects of quality comments as opposed to grades and marks had also been demonstrated in a study by Elawar and Corno (1985), and, as Gordon Stobart (2006) points out, the claim that grades can impede learning is not new. Nearly 100 years ago Edward Lee Thorndike, one of the architects of behaviourism, noted that grades are not a good feedback mechanism because they make, often invidious, comparisons and lack specificity.

Neither of the two extreme marking practices described above would have assisted pupils in knowing where they are, where they need to go or how to get there. They may have sent damaging even if unintended messages to the learners, and are likely to have had negative effects on learning. However, many teachers have developed their marking in line with the principles of assessment for learning and effective feedback, so that the practices described above are becoming rarer. They put the principles into practice in different ways, but the best practice has some common features:

- Teachers are selective in their marking – deciding which pieces of work to give particular attention and which aspects of the work to focus on.
- Teachers identify successes related to the learning intention, pointing out particular parts of the work or making specific comments about it as a whole.
- They use comments only, not a grade or a mark, nor anything else that could be interpreted as such, for example a 'sticker', a 'smiley face' or a merit.
- Teachers indicate progress by referring to the pupil's previous work.
- They specify something that could be improved, or the next steps to take, and give guidance on how to do so.
- Pupils understand the feedback, are clear about what it means and what they have to do.
- Time is routinely made available for pupils to work on their improvement points.
- Teachers work together to improve the quality of their feedback, and value quality above quantity.
- Pupils contribute to, and sometimes initiate, commentary and reflection on their work.

National curriculum levels were designed for summative assessment, providing a general judgement about a pupil's attainment across a broad area of learning. It is not helpful to learning to apply levels, even if subdivided, to particular pieces of work. As guidance from the Qualifications and Curriculum Authority and the national literacy strategy state:

> ... level related judgements should be made only periodically – perhaps once or twice a year. Inspiring teaching ... accompanied by sensitive approaches to assessing and target setting, is much more likely to result in higher standards than measuring progress too frequently.
>
> (QCA, 2003: 1)

Supporting improvement and learning

The notion of improvement, often conceived as closing the gap between present and desired performance, is central to learning, assessment for learning and feedback. Improvement is framed in terms of building on success, rather than correcting mistakes, and practice is developing of pupils making an improvement to the current piece of work, rather than being exhorted 'next time remember to ...'. Improvement is underpinned by the idea of scaffolding learning (Wood *et al*, 1976), where pupils are given just enough assistance to enable them to succeed now, so that in future they can manage with less help and eventually be independent in that area of learning. The process can be thought of as working within the 'zone of proximal development' (Vygotsky, 1987) with the goal just within the pupil's 'extended grasp' (Sutton, 1995: 22). Judging the nature and amount of scaffolding necessary is a delicate task. Clarke (2003) suggests different forms of assistance, including a straightforward reminder of the original learning intention, a broad open question, a focused question, a sentence to complete, a choice of alternatives and an invitation to proffer a new idea. Different prompts can lead to a variety of improvements, for example:

- extension (taking an idea further)
- addition (bringing in a new idea)
- elaboration (by providing more detail or justification)
- amendment (of a phrase, an idea, or by summarizing)
- replacement (of a word, phrase or idea)
- deletion (of something that is superfluous or repetitious)
- correction (generally of spelling, grammar, punctuation or layout, but used sparingly).

Making improvement to the current piece of work is, in most circumstances, an important consideration. For it to be effective in supporting learning, there must be an established process that helps pupils work on their improvements (perhaps at the beginning of the next lesson). Most importantly, the teacher needs to acknowledge the improvement effort, and to make explicit how it relates to the original learning intention or 'horizon of possibilities'. Reflecting on this, a teacher in one of the 'AfL 8 schools project' commented: 'When we started to do this we didn't always check back on the pupil responses but we've tried to tighten this up. We had been teaching too much and not concentrating on the quality of learning' (DfES, 2007: 29).

Whilst the dominant conception of improvement is the next steps on a given learning trajectory, it is timely to recall that other less unidirectional learning journeys are possible, sometimes desirable, and probably the norm away from structured school situations. Learning involves not only improving something and moving towards a given goal, but also revisiting, going deeper, approaching something from a different angle and making new connections. For some students with special educational needs and degenerative conditions, slow regression is a major achievement.

Culture and context

The nature and quality of feedback help create the classroom culture, which in turn influences feedback – its focus, form, status and role in the learning process. If feedback is geared towards improving learning rather than measuring it, if it puts the emphasis on each pupil's progress and avoids comparison among pupils, if it is part of ongoing dialogue rather than a judgement delivered by the teacher after the event and if there is the expectation that feedback is acted upon, it is likely that feedback will make a positive contribution to learning rather than a negative one. In classrooms where these practices become the norm, pedagogy evolves; teachers' and students' self-images change; relationships mature. Testimony from teachers involved in the King's Medway Oxfordshire Formative Assessment Project illustrates profound changes in classroom culture precipitated by teachers taking a thoughtful approach to developing assessment for learning (Black *et al.*, 2003).

The predominant culture of the classroom will affect how pupils receive and respond to feedback. Kluger and DeNisi (1996) identified four ways in which learners react to information about a gap between actual and sought-after standards. They may increase their effort, raise or lower the standard aimed for, abandon the goal or reject the feedback and deny that a gap exists. If the classroom culture is one where making an effort, finding something difficult and learning from mistakes are all accepted and celebrated, pupils are more likely to respond to feedback in ways that help their learning rather than giving up or going into denial. Language is a strong influence on classroom culture, and teachers who are conscious of this deliberately shape the culture by choosing what they say quietly to individual pupils and what they say for the whole class to hear. Shirley Clarke (2003) has found strong links between teachers' language and classroom culture.

The broader context may also affect feedback. For example, where teachers are under great pressure to raise pupils' test scores there may be a tendency for their feedback to be more judgemental than formative. In the Learning How to Learn project Mary James and colleagues found that some teachers emphasized pupils' performance (often in terms of doing well in tests) while others had more of a learning orientation (James *et al.*, 2007).

Many teachers have created classrooms where the culture is of everyone learning, including the teacher. Feedback is not only from teacher to pupils, or among pupils through peer and self-assessment, but also from pupils to teacher. These teachers seek their pupils' perspectives and respond accordingly in order to assist learning. Often feedback from pupils to teachers is in the dialogue and flow of the lesson (as discussed by Jeremy Hodgen and Mary Webb in their chapter). Some teachers ask students to use 'traffic lights' in the form of coloured cards on their desks to provide ongoing feedback on the lesson and their learning. A similar traffic light system can be used by pupils in their books to review learning, while other students write comments to their teachers on their work. In some classrooms the learning culture has developed to the point where feedback from students to the teacher is a natural part of lessons, and a student feels able to put up his hand and say, 'Sir, this isn't working is it?' (Black *et al.*, 2003: 97).

Conclusion

Feedback can be incredibly powerful and is a very strong indicator of what we regard as important, so we need to ensure that feedback reflects our values. Feedback is conceived differently and has different functions in different models of learning, so we need to ensure that feedback is aligned with the kinds of learning that students experience. Feedback is a direct way of making learning explicit, and it has a large part to play in helping pupils become more autonomous learners, and supporting their development of agency. However, it is not simply the existence of feedback that is so influential – it is its nature and quality that is important. No feedback at all would be better than poorly judged or inappropriate feedback since it can have a strong negative effect. Fortunately we now know a substantial amount about the features of effective feedback – feedback that directly supports learning and that creates a classroom culture conducive to learning. Paying attention to the why, who, what, when and how of feedback, taking heed of principles and guidance, and constantly monitoring the actual as opposed to intended effects, will all help ensure that feedback supports rather than frustrates learning and achievement.

Points for reflection

1. Is your feedback helping or hindering learning? What are its actual (as opposed to intended) effects? How could you find out?

2. Review your marking practice against the principles, guidance and suggestions in this chapter. What steps could you take to improve its impact on students' learning?

3. What opportunities can you create for learners to provide you with feedback to inform your teaching?

Further reading

Black, P., Harrison, C., Lee, C., Marshall, B. and Wiliam, D. (2003) *Assessment for Learning: putting it into practice*, Maidenhead: Open University Press.

Clarke, S. (2003) *Enriching Feedback in the Primary Classroom*, Abingdon: Hodder and Stoughton.

—— (2005) *Formative Assessment in Action*, Abingdon: Hodder and Stoughton.

Torrance, H. and Pryor, J. (1998) *Investigating Formative Assessment: teaching, learning and assessment in the classroom*, Maidenhead: Open University Press.

References

ARG (1999) *Assessment for Learning*, Cambridge: University of Cambridge School of Education.

—— (2002a) *Assessment for Learning: 10 principles*. Online, available at: assessment-reform-group.org (accessed 28 May 2007).

—— (2002b) *Testing, Motivation and Learning*, Cambridge: University of Cambridge Faculty of Education.

Askew, S. and Lodge, C. (2000) 'Gifts, ping-pong and loops – linking feedback and learning', in S. Askew (ed.) *Feedback for Learning*, London: RoutledgeFalmer.

Black, P. and Wiliam, D. (1998a) 'Assessment and classroom learning', *Assessment in Education*, 5: 7–71.

—— (1998b) *Inside the Black Box: raising standards through classroom assessment*, London: School of Education, King's College.

Black, P., Harrison, C., Lee, C., Marshall, B. and Wiliam, D. (2003) *Assessment for Learning: putting it into practice*, Maidenhead: Open University Press.

Bredo, D. (1997) 'The social construction of learning', in G.D. Phye (ed.) *Handbook of Academic Learning: construction of social knowledge*, San Diego, CA: Academic Press.

Butler, R. (1988) 'Enhancing and undermining intrinsic motivation: the effects of task-involving and ego-involving evaluation on interest and performance', *British Journal of Educational Psychology*, 58: 1–14.

Clarke, S. (2003) *Enriching Feedback in the Primary Classroom*, Abingdon: Hodder and Stoughton.

—— (2005a) *Formative Assessment in Action*, Abingdon: Hodder and Stoughton.

—— (2005b) *Formative Assessment in the Secondary Classroom*, Abingdon: Hodder and Stoughton.

DfES (2007) *Assessment for Learning 8 Schools Project Report*, London: DfES.

Dweck, C.S. (1999) *Self-Theories: their role in motivation, personality, personality and development*, Philadelphia, PA: Psychology Press.

—— (2006) *Mindset: the new psychology of success*, New York: Random House.

Eisner, E. (2002) *The Arts and the Creation of Mind*, New Haven and London: Yale University Press.

Elawar, E.C. and Corno, L. (1985) 'A factorial experiment in teachers' written feedback on student homework: changing teacher behaviour a little rather than a lot', *Journal of Educational Psychology*, 77: 162–73.

Gipps, C. (1996) *Assessment for the Millennium: form, function and feedback*, London: Institute of Education.

Hargreaves, E., McCallum, B. and Gipps, C. (2000) 'Teacher feedback strategies in primary classrooms – new evidence', in S. Askew (ed.) *Feedback for Learning*, London: RoutledgeFalmer.

Hattie, J. and Timperley, H. (2007) 'The power of feedback', *Review of Educational Research*, 77: 81–112.

James, M. (1998) *Using Assessment for School Improvement*, Oxford: Heinemann.

—— (2006) 'Assessment, teaching and theories of learning', in J. Gardner (ed.) *Assessment and Learning*, London: Sage.

James, M., Black, P., Carmichael, P., Drummond, M.-J., Fox, A., MacBeath, J., Marshall, B., McCormick, R., Pedder, D., Procter, R., Swaffield, S., Swann, J. and Wiliam, D. (2007) *Improving Learning How to Learn: classrooms, schools and networks*, London: Routledge

Kluger, A.N. and DeNisi, A. (1996) 'The effects of feedback interventions on performance: a historical review, a meta-analysis, and a preliminary feedback intervention theory', *Psychological Bulletin*, 27: 111–26.

Marshall, B. and Drummond, M.-J. (2006) 'How teachers engage with assessment for learning: lessons from the classroom', *Research Papers in Education*, 21: 133–49.

Pollard, A. with Collins, J., Maddock, M., Simco, N., Swaffield, S., Warin, J. and Warwick, P. (2005) *Reflective Teaching: effective and evidence-informed professional practice* (2nd edn), London: Continuum.

QCA (2003) *Marking: making a difference*, London: QCA.

Ramaprasad, A. (1983) 'On the definition of feedback', *Behavioural Science*, 28: 4–13.

Sadler, R. (1989) 'Formative assessment and the design of instructional systems', *Instructional Science*, 18: 119–44.

Senge, P. (1992) *The Fifth Discipline: the art and practice of the learning organization*, New York: Doubleday.

Stobart, G. (2006) 'The validity of formative assessment', in J. Gardner (ed.) *Assessment and Learning*, London: Sage.

Sutton, R. (1995) *Assessment for Learning*, Salford: RS Publications.

Torrance, H. and Pryor, J. (1998) *Investigating Formative Assessment: teaching, learning and assessment in the classroom*, Maidenhead: Open University Press.

Tunstall, P. and Gipps, C. (1996) 'Teacher feedback to young children in formative assessment: a typology', *British Educational Research Journal*, 22: 389–404.

Vollmeyer, R. and Rheinberg, F. (2005) 'A surprising effect of feedback on learning', *Learning and Instruction*, 15: 589–602.

Vygotsky, L. (1987) *The Collected Works of L.S. Vygotsky*, vol. 1, New York: Plenum.

Watkins, C. (2003) *Learning: a sense-maker's guide*, London: Association of Teachers and Lecturers.

Wood, D., Bruner, J.S. and Ross, G. (1976) 'The role of tutoring in problem solving', *Journal of Child Psychology and Psychiatry*, 17: 89–100.

Questioning and dialogue

Jeremy Hodgen and Mary Webb

What makes a good assessment question?

Introduction

Feedback is crucial to successful learning (Black and Wiliam, 1998). Indeed, there is considerable evidence to indicate that providing feedback to students is the most effective form of educational intervention (Hattie, 1999; Wiliam, 2007). But how can a teacher provide feedback to a class of students? Providing feedback to one individual is difficult enough. Providing useful feedback to a class of 30 is even more demanding. One way of doing this is through written feedback, an issue that is tackled by Sue Swaffield in her chapter in this volume. Our focus here is on oral feedback – equally important, yet generally less well developed in classrooms. Arguably oral feedback has a far greater potential than written feedback to influence student learning. Black and Wiliam's (1998) review, for example, indicates the power of talk in giving formative feedback to students. Research on formative assessment carried out at King's College London suggests that teacher questioning is a crucial strategy not only in providing feedback directly to the teacher about students' understanding but also in providing feedback from the teacher to the student and between students themselves (Black *et al.*, 2003). Realizing the potential of oral feedback requires teachers to shift the classroom talk towards a more dialogic style in which these different elements of oral feedback all contribute to student learning. In this chapter, we focus on oral feedback and examine how teachers can use questioning and dialogue to provide such feedback to students.

What does research say about questioning and feedback?

The recent interest in formative assessment, in the UK at least, originates in a substantial review of its effectiveness by Black and Wiliam (1998). In this, they describe the broad characteristics of formative assessment as including the use of rich and challenging tasks, a high quality of classroom discourse and questioning, feedback and the use of self- and peer assessment. In particular, they argue that 'the quality of the interaction [between student and teacher] ... is at the heart of pedagogy' (Black and Wiliam, 1998: 16). Subsequent to this review, the Assessment for Learning Group at King's College London investigated the specifics of formative assessment in a collaborative project with a group of secondary teachers, the King's Medway Oxfordshire Formative Assessment (KMOFA) project (Black *et al.*, 2003). Questioning and dialogue enabled teachers and students to communicate about learning in whole class discussions, small group work and one to one discussions between teacher and student or between two students. Further work into developing formative assessment with primary teachers (Webb and Jones, 2006) has identified thoughtful questioning by teachers and students as crucial for promoting the kind of discussion and dialogue that enables students to understand what they have learnt and what are their next steps in learning.

Teachers do already spend a great deal of time in class asking questions – often the majority of a teacher's interventions are questions or feedback on students' answers. So what could teachers do differently? The research evidence suggests that what distinguishes more effective from less effective oral feedback are the kinds of questions asked and the ways in which these questions are used.

Asking better questions

Much classroom discourse consists of what Bloom (1956) terms low-level questions for which the teacher knows the answer (e.g. asking students to recall facts and procedures: What is 8 times 6? Which button do you press to save the file? What is a solute? Which punctuation mark do we use here?). Generally, increasing the proportion of higher-level questions is associated with increases in student performance (Burton *et al.*, 1986). Higher-order questions require students to think (e.g. 'How would you work out 8 times 6 if you didn't know it?' 'How could yesterday's experiment be improved or extended?' 'In what ways are these two characters similar?'). Such questioning is often focused less on what students already know (although this may be important) and more on what they need to do in order to learn more. But the situation is a complex one. First, the extent to which a question is challenging is dependent on what the students know. A high-level question for one class may be a low-level question for another. In order to generate 'good' questions a teacher needs to know the students. Second, higher-level questions are 'harder'. They require students to construct new knowledge. Generally, higher-order questions require time and space for learners both to engage with the challenge and to generate responses.

Giving students time to think

One strategy for higher-order questions is to increase the wait time (the time between a teacher asking a question and taking an answer). The wait time is typically less than one second in most classrooms. For higher-order questions, increasing wait time to around three seconds can have very dramatic effects on the involvement of students in classroom discussion (Rowe, 1974), including more students contributing, longer student responses, students commenting on each other's ideas and a greater variety of ideas. In addition, this emphasizes the importance of answering and establishes the expectation that students will give thoughtful, reasoned answers.

However, whilst wait time is very powerful, increased wait time is not an effective strategy for lower-order more straightforward questions (e.g. recall of number facts) and solely increasing wait time to more than about five seconds can actually decrease the quality of classroom talk (Tobin, 1986). Indeed, sometimes teachers may think that they are using wait time, when actually the question is at an inappropriate level for the students (Hodgen, 2007). This is illustrated by the following example that occurred during a Year 8 mathematics lesson about straight-line graphs. Having examined a variety of different graphs and equations, the teacher asked:

> Is $y = 3x + 3$ the same as $3x = y - 3$? [Two-second pause] Is $y = 3x + 3$ the same as $3x = y - 3$? [Five-second pause] We're looking $y = 3x + 3$ and $3x = y - 3$. Are they the same? [Two-second pause] Ok. Let's look on the board.

The teacher's repeated and reframed questions took over 20 seconds and contained three pauses or wait times. The central question that the teacher asked is certainly an interesting one and appropriate to Year 8 students. It gave the teacher feedback – the students could not answer the question. Her response to this was to demonstrate the equivalence of the two equations herself. In this case, the wait time gave the students time to think, but the students needed more structure. Indeed, given the students' lack of response to the question, it seems unlikely that many of them understood the teacher's explanation. A different approach might have been to ask the students to discuss the question in pairs, perhaps asking 'Is there anything we've done today, that would help answer this question?' Alternatively, if class time was limited, the teacher might have written the question on the board as a conundrum to be solved at a later date.

Listening to students

One of the most significant changes in the practice of the KMOFA project teachers was in the way they listened to students' responses (Black *et al.*, 2003). At the beginning of the study, teachers listened to students' responses in a way that Davis (1997) calls 'evaluative listening'. They listened for the correct answer, and when students gave partially correct answers, they said things like, 'almost' or 'nearly'. This encouraged the belief that the teacher was more interested in getting students to give the correct answer, rather than finding out what they thought about a particular idea. Over time, the teachers increasingly listened interpretively to the students – they listened to what students said in order to work out why the students had responded in the way they had. What was more, even the students noticed. As one Year 8 girl said, 'When Miss used to ask a question, she used to be interested in the right answer. Now she's interested in what we think.'

The teacher talking less but listening more has a number of benefits for teachers and students. First, listening to students enables teachers themselves to learn more about what students know and how well they know it. Students then realize the teacher is actually interested in what they say and are thus encouraged to say more. Second, when teachers spend less time talking, students' contributions tend to get longer. As a result, students have more opportunities to listen to others' ideas and to compare them with their own. According to Mercer and colleagues (Mercer *et al.*, 2004), when students are actively involved in discussion not only do they learn more, but their general ability actually increases. Finally, talking less gives the teacher more time to think about the interventions she does make. Teacher interventions are crucial in promoting formative assessment, and we are suggesting that these interventions should in general be less frequent but more thoughtful and challenging. Listening enables a teacher to find out what students already know so she can challenge them to extend their knowledge. Alternatively, an intervention might be directed at encouraging students to challenge each other. Of course, posing a question and listening to the students' ideas may demonstrate that students have no difficulty in the area, in which case the teacher would move on. On the other hand it may indicate that a topic needs tackling again, perhaps in a different way.

Responding to students

How teachers respond to students' answers can indicate to students whether the teacher is interested in helping them to learn, how well they are doing, what more they need to learn and how to approach their learning. Thus teachers' responses can create or destroy a productive learning environment. Providing oral feedback is about much more than simply telling students if they are right or wrong. Indeed, telling a student whether their response is correct provides almost no information about what they need to do to learn more. Yet classrooms tend to be dominated by a style of communication in which the majority of feedback is of this very type. Sinclair and Coulthard (1975), for example, found that most classroom dialogue was of an initiation, response, feedback, or IRF, pattern – the teacher asks a question, a student provides an answer, then the teacher informs students whether they have got an answer right or wrong. For example:

Teacher: What is a solute? [No pause]

Pupil: A substance dissolved in a liquid.

Teacher: Good. What is a solvent?

The question is closed – it has a narrow range of acceptable responses. Indeed, the speed of the response suggests that the student simply knew the answer, although it does not provide any information about what this (or the other) students understand by these scientific terms. In this example, crucially, the feedback is also restricted to an indication of whether the student's response is correct or not. An alternative response might have been to invite responses from other students ('what do you think about that answer?') or to focus on the meaning of the terms ('so what does dissolved mean?').

Teachers who have developed their formative whole class interactions to a high level generally end their comments with questions related to students' previous responses, and thus develop the dialogue (Webb and Jones, 2006). Many of the teachers' rejoinders were 'why' or 'how' questions, designed to encourage the students to explain their ideas further. Other questions aimed to involve students by encouraging them to respond to points made by their peers (e.g. 'can anyone help here?'). This is very different from the IRF model discussed above. The teacher does not make a judgement, and encourages other students to continue the dialogue, thus providing opportunities for students to give feedback to each other. In the best examples the dialogue resembles that described by Alexander as 'dialogic teaching' in which there is a 'common understanding through structured, cumulative questioning and discussion which guide and prompt, reduce choices, minimize risk and error, and expedite "handover" of concepts and principles' (Alexander, 2004: 24). Enabling students to use talk effectively in groups to assess what they have learned and to develop their thinking further requires the teacher to model, develop rules and continually encourage students. Mercer described the resulting 'exploratory talk' as:

[Talk] in which partners engage critically but constructively with each other's ideas. Relevant information is offered for joint consideration. Proposals may be challenged and counter-challenged, but if so reasons are given and alternatives are offered. Agreement is sought as a basis for joint progress. Knowledge is made publicly accountable and reasoning is visible in the talk.

(Mercer, 2000: 98)

Teachers' interventions to encourage thinking and to promote useful talk and dialogue depend on listening to students not only to assess what they have learned but also to identify what they have not understand or have only partially grasped. If teachers are simply waiting to hear the 'right answer' they are less likely to gain any useful assessment information. By assessing students in the moment of classroom talk, teachers can make in the moment decisions about appropriate responses and strategies (Perrenoud, 1998). In a small group discussion their decision might focus on how best to respond to a student so as to promote thinking, perhaps by probing understanding further. In a class discussion an individual student's needs have to be balanced with those of the whole class. These potentially conflicting needs can be reconciled within a culture where mistakes and misunderstanding are perceived as essential opportunities for learning, and students feel responsible not only for their own learning but also for supporting that of other students (Webb and Jones, 2006). Where such a culture is established the teacher may choose, during a whole class discussion, to probe students' thinking and use a misconception as a learning opportunity, or to move the discussion forward while mentally noting individuals' difficulties. If teachers are to be responsive to students' learning needs they must listen to students, then tailor the classroom activity to these needs. This is likely to involve, at least in some cases, departing from the prepared lesson plan. Hence teaching involves two levels of planning or decision making: designing tasks, activities and lessons in advance, and the moment-by-moment adaptation of activities on the basis of feedback from students (Perrenoud, 1998).

Questioning, dialogue and feedback in action: two lessons

In the following extracts from two class discussions, the first in history and the second in mathematics, we explore how questioning and dialogue can be used in practice to promote feedback.[1]

Extract 1: a history lesson

The first extract centres on a discussion of how to arrange pictures (identified by letters) relating to the slave trade. The teacher has asked which picture comes at the start of the sequence.

Shari:	Is it B, because they're loading things from England to take to Africa?
Teacher:	What things?
Shari:	Like er cloth and things like that to trade with the slaves and that.

Teacher:	It certainly is a boat being loaded up OK. That can be one viewpoint. So hold that viewpoint. Is anyone going to challenge that viewpoint? I like your idea there. Well justified! Well done! James?
James:	Is it C because the slaves have just been caught and they're going to be traded and sold?
Teacher:	Right. OK. The slaves have just been caught. Anyone going to help out James?
Becky:	We said D because it looks like they've just been kind of like attacked and taken from their village. And then C.
Teacher:	That is the point we were discussing a minute or two ago OK? Wayne can you give her a hand?
Stephen:	I was going to argue with Becky because on Picture D the Americans have got guns so that means they must ….
Teacher:	Sorry – the who? Not Americans?
Stephen:	Oh – Africans.
Teacher:	Yes.
Stephen:	Have got guns so that must mean that they must have traded the slaves already for the guns.
Teacher:	Why else can we decide that Picture D isn't really going to be the start? Because what are they trying to achieve in Picture D? David?
David:	They're killing the slaves and they're meant to be capturing them.
Teacher:	Right a dead slave is a no good slave. John?
John:	I think it's B because B looks like they're leaving from a proper port in England.
Teacher:	OK. Right. I mean either way it doesn't matter. What matters is justification. So either way it's good. What I would say to you though is that in the group discussions I think we've decided now haven't we that Picture D actually isn't the start point because they have got rifles there.

Of particular note is that in contrast to the dominant IRF style discussed above, the teacher's interventions initiate further responses from students. Certainly, he gave feedback to the students, but in ways that opened up discussion. Only in his final and ninth contribution does he conclude the discussion. The teacher's interventions shifted the talk towards what Alexander (2004) classifies as dialogue, because the structured, cumulative questioning and discussion promotes a developing understanding of what is necessary for justification. Rather than giving simple feedback the teacher encouraged the students to respond to each other's viewpoints, extend each other's ideas and challenge each other – in other words to give each other feedback.

Points for reflection

1   In what ways and to what extent did the teacher's intervention encourage feedback from the students themselves?

2   What messages are the teacher's responses likely to give to the students about their contributions to the discussion?

3   How is this discussion similar or different from discussions in your classroom?

4   If you were teaching this lesson, what changes would you make to the teacher's interventions and questions?

Extract 2: a mathematics lesson

The following extract took place during the first lesson in a sequence on percentages. The teacher's purpose was explicitly formative: for herself and the students themselves to find out what the students knew about percentages to inform subsequent lessons. She had asked a pair of students to discuss an (incorrect) idea that had arisen in their discussion[2]:

Terri: We think 5 per cent is like 10 per cent doubled but we're not sure.

Student: Because if you say it as fractions, 5 per cent is one-twentieth and 10 per cent is one-tenth and then if you do one-twentieth doubled, it would be one-tenth.

Teacher: OK. Anybody want to say anything about that?

Student: I'm confused.

Teacher: OK. Well if you're confused you need to ask her a question. Girls you need to help her, it's your group. It's not just Terri.

Student:	Could you repeat what you said again because I think I mis-heard.
Terri:	We thought that 5 per cent was 10 per cent doubled.
Teacher:	I'll write that down [teacher writes '5% is 10% doubled' on the board].
Students:	'Is that right?'; 'How's that?'; '10 per cent is 5 per cent doubled?'; '10 per cent is 5 per cent doubled'; '10 per cent doubled is …?' [in pairs/groups, simultaneously]
Teacher:	First thing then. Have I written down what you said?
Student:	Yeah.
Student:	Yeah.
Student:	I thought 10 per cent doubled was 20 per cent …'cos if you have 100, 10 per cent would be like ten, and 5 per cent would be like five, 10 per cent doubled would be 20, 20 per cent.
Student:	Is it supposed to be 5 per cent is 10 per cent halved not doubled?
Teacher:	Do you think it is? Instead of saying is it supposed to be, what do you think?
Student:	I think … 10 per cent doubled is 20 per cent.
Student:	I'm not too sure about this but I think I don't agree with sort of what she said because it's like a divide. Isn't it sort of like a divide sum?
Teacher:	Could you tell us a bit more about what you mean?
Student:	Say if you had five and if you divided it by 20, that'd be four, I mean if you had ten it'd be two … oh yeah, it doesn't matter.
Teacher:	Why doesn't it matter?
Student:	Because I've just worked something out and it is 10 per cent is supposed to be 5 per cent doubled.
Teacher:	You've listened to lots of things. Are you going to stick with it or …?

We note that this discussion actually went on for a further 20 minutes during which the teacher probed how the students justified how they 'knew' that '5 per cent is 10 per cent doubled' or vice versa. It was only at the very end of this extended discussion that she gave feedback that the correct statement is '10 per cent is 5 per cent doubled'. We think that it is particularly significant that the teacher focused on an incorrect idea as if it could be correct. In her final contribution in this extract, she had the opportunity to close down the discussion, but instead she asked the pupils to decide on which was correct. By doing this, she was able to examine the students' underlying understandings of percentages in some depth – and through the discussion enabled the students themselves to get feedback and to respond directly to each other. As this excerpt demonstrates, the use of such provocative statements can be very valuable in promoting discussion (Dillon, 1990).

Points for reflection

1. In what ways and to what extent did the teacher's intervention encourage feedback and discussion between the students themselves?
2. How could the teacher's interventions and questions be adapted for another lesson or school subject?
3. How would you plan for a discussion in which students responded directly to each other?

Designing questions and encouraging dialogue

We now turn to focus on more practical strategies for using questioning and talk. There are two broad aspects to teachers' questioning: initiating activities and responding to students. When planning activities, teachers do of course need to anticipate how students may respond and to generate appropriate interventions and questions. Questions 'work' if they challenge students, but the extent to which students are challenged depends very much on their existing knowledge. Good questioning is very much contingent on what actually happens in classroom interaction. Hence, realizing the potential of good questions or activities depends largely on a teacher's moment-by-moment decisions during classroom interactions and discussions. Whilst there is no such thing as a universally good question, our work with teachers has demonstrated the value of a number of generic question types. We consider these in three broad categories: starters and prompts; encouraging feedback from students; and ways of involving all students. (See Further Reading below for more advice and ideas about questions.)

Starters and prompts

The following questions encourage students to think about the problem or task they are working on, to consider the issues in relation to their previous experience and to come up with ideas. They tend to open up the discussion because there are generally plenty of appropriate answers, so a key role for the teacher is to enable as many students as possible to be involved in thinking and discussion.

- Tell me about the problem.
- What do you know about the problem? Can you describe the problem to someone else?
- Have you seen a problem like this before?
- What is similar ...? What is different ...?
- Do you have a hunch? ... a conjecture?
- What would happen if ...? Is it always true that ...?
- How do you know that ...? Can you justify ...? Can you find a different method?
- Can you explain ... improve/add to that explanation ...?
- What have you found out? What advice would you give to someone else about ...?
- What was easy/difficult about this task?

These generic questions are only starting points and in most cases a question 'works' best when tailored to the particular context. But open-ended questions are generally more productive, challenging and interesting than closed questions. As Philip, one of the teachers from the KMOFA project, put it:

> Nowadays, when we start a new unit, we start by looking at what we already know. This might be by having an in depth question and answer session − with open-ended, challenging questions − such as, 'If plants need sunlight to make food how come the biggest plants don't grow in deserts, where it's sunny all the time?' A far better lead in to the recall of photo-synthesis than 'What is the equation for photosynthesis?'. The former question allows all those students who don't even remember the word photosynthesis to begin formulating ideas, and to be part of a discussion which gradually separates those who do remember and understand photo-synthesis, from those who don't.
>
> (Black *et al.*, 2003: 35)

Encouraging discussion

As we have already noted, one strategy to encourage discussion is simply for the teacher to say less. This gives students more opportunity to think about and comment on each other's ideas. Sometimes, however, students need more struc-tured thinking and discussion prompts. These questions and statements can be used to encourage contributions that expand or clarify ideas:

- Can you put Moinul's idea into your own words?
- What could you add to Hannah's answer?
- If you're not sure, you could ask Ruby a question.
- Can anyone improve Stuart's answer?
- Which parts of Rahima's answer would you agree with?

Ways of involving all students

For questioning to be effective, all students need to contribute to classroom discussion, but teachers often find that the same high attaining students make the majority of contributions. A 'no hands up' strategy can help avoid this and establish a classroom culture in which all students are expected to contribute. If a student responds 'I don't know', an effective strategy can be to say, 'OK, I'll come back to you.' After the teacher has collected answers from other students, she can return to the first student and ask which of the answers is best. In this way, the student has a positive role to play – she needs to listen to other students and engage in the activity. In classrooms where the habit of expecting students to answer and giving them time to think was established students were more prepared to try even when they were unsure of the answer.

Discussion in small groups generally enables all students to engage directly in larger group discussion and respond to questions. This assists students in understanding the problem better and in clarifying their own ideas. In turn, a greater number of students contribute to whole class discussions and their contributions are better articulated. We suggest that frequent but short whole class discussions balanced with small group discussions can be very effective. Other strategies for enabling students to engage with the discussion and to encourage well-formed answers include the following.

- Give students time to prepare for a discussion. Ways of doing this include giving students an opportunity to discuss a task or problem with a partner, rehearsing their contribution with the teacher or a classroom assistant, or making some notes to use as an aide-memoire.
- Give students time to think. When students make a higher-order contribution – whether as a new idea or a question – give the other students wait time before taking responses. Alternatively ask students to discuss the idea or question in pairs.
- Give students time to think about and disagree with an idea even if it is correct: e.g. 'Femi suggested that we use a database to implement this system. Are there any other possible applications that you think might be better?'
- Support students to develop good questions. Discuss with students the questions they use themselves.

Our research suggests that discussion in which all students contribute openly is vital to effective formative feedback. Students can at times be reluctant to give answers that they think may be incorrect. Hence teachers need to value all contributions – mistakes and partially correct answers included – and encourage students to challenge any ideas they disagree with or do not understand.

- Invite students to express partial ideas or hunches even if they can't completely articulate them. They, or other students, can then amend or adapt the ideas.
- Record all contributions on the board. Invite comments, or ask students in pairs to identify one idea they disagree with or do not understand. They can then ask for clarification or explanation in whole class discussion.
- Challenge correct as well as incorrect answers. Ask students to justify their ideas: 'How do you know …?' and ask other students to comment: 'What do you think about …?' Thus students are asked to think about how as well as what they know.
- Value students' mistakes and errors. One important way of doing this is to record and discuss all ideas. Or focus on one partial idea and ask, 'What made that idea a sensible conjecture?'
- Demonstrate that you are interested in what students say. Be prepared to deviate from your lesson plan to concentrate on an unexpected or tricky issue. If there is no time for this, or the students cannot find a satisfactory response, record the problem and return to it at a later date.
- Practise ways of avoiding letting students know whether an answer is correct through body language, facial expression or type of comment.

One useful technique is for a teacher to make a mistake deliberately. This can be an opportunity to ensure that the class discuss a particular problematic idea, as in the maths vignette above. If students spot the mistake, this provides an opportunity for a student to correct the teacher and provide an explanation in their own words. If the students don't notice it, the teacher could highlight it herself: 'Oh, that looks wrong, is it?' or 'Oh dear, I've made a mistake. Can anyone spot what I've done wrong?' Giving students responsibility for identifying and correcting mistakes in this way encourages an attitude that what matters is the ideas themselves rather than whether the person saying them is 'clever' or not.

Putting it into practice

A teacher on the Jersey Actioning Formative Assessment Project who had been leading professional development in her school reflected:

85

I think questioning has been difficult because everybody does it to a level. Teachers naturally question but I think a lot of the time people have ignored the fact that there hasn't been an answer and they feed the answers in or they're wanting a particular response so they're answering for the children rather than saying 'OK let's wait for a little bit' and just see what happens. And I think people say 'well I don't need to plan questions because it's what we do' but I think if you want to move learning deeper you need to think about the kind of questions and why you are asking them.

As this teacher commented, questioning is not easy to develop partly because teachers are already doing it. But, as one of the KMOFA project teachers put it, it is 'not until you analyse your own questioning do you realize how poor it can be' (Black *et al.*, 2003: 51). Responsive questioning, that is responding in the moment to students' ideas, is very complex. There is no easy resolution but there is a great deal of evidence that sharing, talking about and reflecting upon questioning with other teachers is a very valuable way for teachers to increase their repertoire of questions, as well as their ability to use these questions in the classroom. A group of teachers who will be teaching the same topic could:

- Brainstorm some questions to use at the start of the lesson.
- Choose a few of the questions that might be more useful for formative assessment.
- Try to predict the type and range of answers the students might give.
- Discuss how to respond to those answers and what to do next.
- In pairs observe each other's lessons on the topic making notes of (or audio record with permission) the questions and answers and any other evidence of students' learning.
- Discuss the evidence of how well students were learning and consider how the questions and follow-up enabled (or otherwise) students' learning.
- Discuss any possible revisions to the plan or the responses.
- Observe each other teach – or team teach the lesson. Alternatively, make an audio recording.
- After the lesson, discuss: what sorts of questions did you use? what styles of dialogue are evident in your classroom? what opportunities are there to adopt some of the strategies outlined in this chapter?

The changes that we are proposing here are neither easy nor quick to implement, but they are of immense value in terms of students' learning, as well as providing feedback on the teaching itself.

We conclude with two teachers from the KMOFA project (Black *et al.*, 2003) talking about the necessity and benefits of analysing and improving questioning:

I'd become dissatisfied with the closed Q&A style that my unthinking teaching had fallen into, and I would frequently be lazy in my acceptance of right answers and sometimes even tacit complicity with a class to make sure none of us had to work too hard. […] They and I knew that if the Q&A wasn't going smoothly, I'd change the question, answer it myself or only seek answers from the 'brighter students'. There must have been times (still are?) where an outside observer would see my lessons as a small discussion group surrounded by many sleepy onlookers.

(Black *et al.*, 2003: 48)

[I] really started to think about the type of questions I was asking – were they just instant one word answers, what were they testing – knowledge or understanding, was I giving the class enough time to answer the question, was I quickly accepting the correct answer, was I asking the girl to explain her answer, how was I dealing with the wrong answer? When I really stopped to think I realized that I could make a very large difference to the girls' learning by using all their answers to govern the pace and content of the lesson.

(Black *et al.*, 2003: 50)

Notes

1. These two lessons originate from the 'Questioning, dialogue and assessment for learning' video project funded by the Department for Education and Skills in 2004. The names used are pseudonyms. The lessons themselves are discussed in more depth elsewhere: the history lesson in Black *et al.* (in preparation), and the mathematics lesson in Hodgen and Marshall (2005).
2. The correct statement is that 10 per cent is 5 per cent doubled or alternatively 5 per cent is 10 per cent halved; 5 per cent = five-hundredths or one-twentieth; 10 per cent = ten-hundredths or two-twentieths. This relates to a common misconception about fractions, that one-tenth is double one-fifth. Actually one-fifth is double one-tenth.

Further reading

The Black Box series of pamphlets contain useful information and advice on questioning both in general and specifically in relation to specific subjects: *Inside the Black Box* (Black and Wiliam), *Working Inside the Black Box* (Black, Harrison, Lee, Marshall and Wiliam), *English Inside the Black Box* (Marshall and Wiliam), *Mathematics Inside the Black Box* (Hodgen and Wiliam), *ICT Inside the Black Box* (Webb and Cox), *Science Inside the Black Box* (Black and Harrison) are all available from nferNelson: online, available at: www.nfer-nelson.co.uk/ (accessed 11 July 2007).

Other useful reading includes:

Alexander, R.J. (2004) *Towards Dialogic Teaching: rethinking classroom talk*, York: Dialogos.

Assessment Reform Group (2006) *The Role of Teachers in the Assessment of Learning*, London: ARG.

Black, P.J., Harrison, C., Lee, C., Marshall, B. and Wiliam, D. (2003) *Assessment for Learning: putting it into practice*, Buckingham: Open University Press.

Brooks, R. and Tough, S. (2006) *Assessment and Testing: making space for teaching and learning*, London: Institute for Public Policy Research.

Brown, G. and Wragg, E.C. (1993) *Questioning*, London: Routledge.

Dillon, J.T. (1990) *The Practice of Questioning*, London: Routledge.

Dweck, C.S. (2007) 'Learn to leave that evil twin behind', *Times Higher Educational Supplement*, 1 June: 14.

Gardner, J. (ed.) (2006) *Assessment and Learning*, London: Sage.

Mercer, N. (1995) *The Guided Construction of Knowledge: talk among teachers and learners*, Clevedon: Multilingual Matters Ltd.

Naylor, S. and Keogh, B. (2007) 'Active assessment: thinking, learning and assessment in science', *School Science Review*, 88: 73–9.

Scott, P. and Ametller, J. (2007) 'Teaching science in a meaningful way: striking a balance between "opening up" and "closing down" classroom talk', *School Science Review*, 88: 77–83.

Suffolk LEA (2001) 'How Do they Walk on Hot Sand? Using questions to develop learning', online, available at: www.slamnet.org.uk/assessment/index.htm (accessed 11 July 2007).

Watson, A. and Mason, J. (1998) *Questions and Prompts for Mathematical Thinking*, Derby: Association of Teachers of Mathematics.

References

Alexander, R.J. (2004) *Towards Dialogic Teaching: rethinking classroom talk*, York: Dialogos.

Black, P. and Wiliam, D. (1998) 'Assessment and classroom learning', *Assessment in Education*, 5: 7–74.

Black, P.J., Harrison, C., Lee, C., Marshall, B. and Wiliam, D. (2003) *Assessment for Learning: putting it into practice*, Buckingham: Open University Press.

Black, P., Harrison, C., Hodgen, J., Marshall, B. and Webb, M (in preparation) Pedagogy and subject cultures: the specifics of formative assessment. Unpublished manuscript.

Bloom, B.S. (1956) *Taxonomy of Educational Objectives*, New York: Longman.

Burton, J.K., Niles, J.A., Lalik, R.M. and Reed, W.M. (1986) 'Cognitive capacity engagement during and following interspersed mathemagenic question', *Journal of Educational Psychology*, 78: 147–52.

Davis, B. (1997) 'Listening for differences: an evolving conception of mathematics teaching', *Journal for Research in Mathematics Education*, 28: 355–76.

Dillon, J.T. (1990) *The Practice of Questioning*, London: Routledge.

Hattie, J. (1999) 'Influences on student learning', Inaugural Professorial Lecture, August. Online, available at: www.education.auckland.ac.nz/uoa/education/staff/j.hattie/papers/influences.cfm (accessed 15 May 2007).

Hodgen, J. (2007) 'Formative assessment: tools for transforming school mathematics towards dialogic practice?' Paper presented at the CERME 5: Fifth Congress of the European Society for Research in Mathematics Education, Larnaca, Cyprus.

Hodgen, J. and Marshall, B. (2005) 'Assessment for learning in English and mathematics: a comparison', *Curriculum Journal*, 16: 153–76.

Mercer, N. (2000) *Words and Minds: how we use language to think together*, London: Routledge.

Mercer, N., Dawes, L., Wegerif, R. and Sams, C. (2004) 'Reasoning as a scientist: ways of helping children to use language to learn science', *British Educational Research Journal*, 30: 359–77.

Perrenoud, P. (1998) 'From formative assessment to a controlled regulation of learning processes: towards a wider conceptual field', *Assessment in Education*, 5: 85–102.

Rowe, M.B. (1974) 'Wait time and rewards as instructional variables, their influence on language, logic and fate control', *Journal of Research in Science Teaching*, 11: 91–4.

Sinclair, J.M. and Coulthard, R.M. (1975) *Towards an Analysis of Discourse: the English used by teachers and pupils*, London: Oxford University Press.

Tobin, K. (1986) 'Effects of teacher wait time on discourse characteristics in mathematics and language arts classes', *American Educational Research Journal*, 23: 191–200.

Webb, M.E. and Jones, J. (2006) 'Assessment for learning transforming classroom practice?', Paper presented at the British Educational Research Association Annual Conference, University of Warwick, September.

Wiliam, D. (2007) 'Assessment for learning: why, what and how?' Professorial lecture, Institute of Education, University of London, April.

Getting to the core of learning

Using assessment for self-monitoring and self-regulation

Lorna Earl and Steven Katz

All young people need to become their own best self-assessors.

Pupils in modern society are living in confusing and unpredictable times, in which they must be equipped with skills that enable them to think for themselves and be self-initiating, self-modifying and self-directing. They must acquire the capacity to learn and change consciously, continuously and quickly, to anticipate what might happen and continually search for more creative solutions. Learning for the twenty-first century involves much more than acquiring knowledge. It requires the capacity for 'reflective judgment' – the ability to make judgements and interpretations, less on the basis of 'right answers' than on the basis of 'good reasons' (King and Kitchener, 1994).

Delors *et al.* (1996), in their powerful work for UNESCO *Learning: the treasure within*, identified four essential pillars of learning – learning to know, learning to do, learning to live together and learning to be – a testament to the growing need for informed, skilled and compassionate citizens who value truth, openness, creativity, interdependence, balance and love, as well as the search for personal and spiritual freedom in all areas of one's life. This image of learning means fundamental changes in orientations to teaching and learning in schools. It means that schools must become places that foster high-level learning for all students in all of these domains.

Assessment has the potential to be a key element in transforming schools into places of high quality learning for all students. Why? Because assessment can be one of the most powerful processes that schools and teachers have to prepare students for the future in all of the domains in the UNESCO framework.

Assessment for learning

Since the ground-breaking work of Terry Crooks (1988), Black and Wiliam (1998a, 1998b) and the Assessment Reform Group (1999), assessment for learning has taken hold worldwide as a high leverage approach to school improvement. In assessment for learning we have a pedagogical approach that has the potential, at least, to influence student learning. But, as many authors have told us, assessment for learning is not a 'quick fix'. For teachers really to engage in assessment for learning requires a lot of new professional learning and it requires changes in how teachers interact with their pupils, how they think about the material they teach and, most importantly, how they use assessment in their daily work. Much of this volume is focused on helping teachers understand assessment for learning better – both the theory on which it is based and the practical processes that make it work.

In this chapter, we aim to provide teachers with a deeper understanding of the ways that assessment can help pupils become thoughtful, self-monitoring and self-regulating learners. Assessment for learning is based on a complex set of ideas and theories and provides a model for teachers to use assessment to rethink, revise and refine their teaching. It also assists them in the provision of feedback, and to focus on creating the conditions for pupils to become confident and competent self-assessors. In our experience with teachers who are engaging in assessment for learning, they are often preoccupied with using assessment to inform their teaching decisions and provide feedback to students. Sometimes the feedback gives students the raw materials for becoming better at self-assessment. However, teachers rarely think proactively about what they need to do to use assessment to promote student self-assessment and self-regulation so that students become adept at defining their own learning goals and monitoring their progress towards them.

This chapter is concerned with this second dimension of assessment for learning, emphasising the role of the pupil as the critical connector between assessment and learning. We have called this 'assessment as learning' (Earl, 2003; Earl and Katz, 2005) – the kind of assessment that recognises students as active, engaged and critical assessors who make sense of information, relate it to prior knowledge and use it for new learning. This is the regulatory process in metacognition, in which students personally monitor what they are learning and use the feedback from this monitoring to make adjustments, adaptations and even major changes in what they understand. When teachers focus on assessment as learning they use classroom assessment as the vehicle for helping pupils develop, practise and become comfortable with reflection and with critical analysis of their own learning. Viewed this way, self-assessment and meaningful learning are inextricably linked.

In this chapter, we expand on this notion of assessment as learning by showing how it relates to current learning theory and by describing teachers' roles in developing reflection and self-regulation in their pupils.

Assessment and learning

How People Learn: Brain, Mind, Experience and School, the seminal synthesis of literature in the cognitive and developmental sciences produced by the National Research Council in the USA (Bransford *et al.*, 1999), identified three principles that underpin how people learn:

1.   Students come to the classroom with preconceptions about how the world works. If their understanding is not engaged, they may fail to grasp the new concepts and information, or they may learn them for purposes of the test but revert to their preconceptions outside the classroom.

2.   To develop competence in an area of inquiry, student must have a deep foundation of factual knowledge, understand facts and ideas in the context of a conceptual framework, and organise knowledge in ways that facilitate retrieval and application.

3.   A 'metacognitive' approach to instruction can help students learn to take control of their own learning by defining learning goals and monitoring their progress in achieving them.

These principles portray learning as an interactive process by which learners try to make sense of new information and integrate it into what they already know. Students are always thinking and they are either challenging or reinforcing their thinking on a moment-by-moment basis.

Before teachers can plan for targeted teaching and classroom activities they need to have a sense of what it is that pupils are thinking. What is it that they believe to be true? This process involves much more than 'Do they have the right or wrong answer?' It means making pupils' thinking visible and understanding the images and patterns that they have constructed in order to make sense of the world from their perspective (Earl, 2003). It means using this information to provide scaffolding for the learner to create new connections, and attach these connections to a conceptual framework that allows efficient and effective retrieval and use of the new information.

The following anecdote gives a vivid description of how this learning process happens, and the critical role that assessment plays in the learning process.

When she was about five years old my niece Joanna (Jojo to the family) came up to me and announced that: 'All cats are girls and all dogs are boys.' When I asked her why she believed cats were girls and dogs were boys, she responded: 'Your cat Molly is a girl and she's little and smooth, girls are little and smooth, too. Cats are girls. The dog next door is a boy and he's big and rough, just like boys are big and rough. Dogs are boys.' Clearly, she had identified a problem, surveyed her environment, gathered data, formulated a hypothesis and, when she tested it, it held. Pretty sophisticated logic for a five-year-old.

I pulled a book about dogs from my bookshelf and showed her a picture of a chihuahua, a dog that was little and smooth.

'What's this?' I asked.

'Dog', she replied.

'Girl or boy?'

'It's a boy, dogs are boys.'

'But it's little and smooth', I pointed out.

'Sometimes they can be little and smooth', said Jojo.

I turned to a picture of an Irish setter, surrounded by puppies. She was perturbed.

'What's this?'

'Dog', she replied, with some hesitation.

'Boy or girl?'

After a long pause she said, 'Maybe it's the dad.' But she didn't look convinced and she quickly asked: 'Can dogs be girls, Aunt Lorna?'

This anecdote is a simple but vivid demonstration of the process of assessment, feedback, reflection and self-monitoring that we all use when we are trying to make sense of the world around us. Jojo had a conception (or hypothesis) about something in her world (the gender of cats and dogs). She had come to a conclusion based on her initial investigation that held with her experience. With the intervention of a teacher (Aunt Lorna) who used assessment (How do you know?) and created the conditions (the picture book) for her to compare her conceptions with other examples in the real world, she was able to see the gap between her understanding and other evidence. Once she had the new knowledge, she moved quickly to adjust her view and consider alternative perspectives.

This kind of assessment is at the core of helping pupils become aware of and take control of their own learning. And it is this kind of assessment that supports the type of learning that psychologists describe as conceptual change. Rather than transforming evidence that exists in the world to fit established mental structures (conceptions), the mental structures themselves shift (or accommodate) to take new evidence into account. Classroom assessment, in this view, promotes the learner's accommodation process. It is something best – and necessarily – accomplished by the learner herself since it is she who holds privileged access to the relevant beliefs, though as we saw above, the teacher's role is to help make them public (Katz, 2000).

Assessment as learning

Assessment as learning is premised on the need for all young people to become their own best self-assessors. Why? Because self-assessment is the third fundamental principle of how people learn (Bransford *et al.*, 1999). Although the first two principles identified above are key ingredients of good pedagogy and enhanced learning, the third principle is the one that underpins self-awareness and life-long learning – creating the conditions to develop metacognitive awareness so that they have the skills and habits to monitor and regulate their own learning. Metacognition, as defined by Brown (1987) has two dimensions – 'knowledge of cognition' (knowledge about ourselves as learners and what influences our performance; knowledge about learning strategies; knowledge about when and why to use a strategy) and 'regulation of cognition' (planning – setting goals and activating relevant background knowledge; regulation – monitoring and self-testing; evaluation – appraising the products and regulatory processes of learning).

Metacognition means that pupils must become reflective about their own learning, a skill that like all complex learning requires years of practice, concentration and coaching. It does not have a beginning and an end but rather continues to develop and to be honed across disciplines and contexts (Costa, 2006). And it doesn't happen by chance. If pupils are to become metacognitive thinkers and problem solvers who can bring their talents and their knowledge to bear on their decisions and actions, they have to develop these skills of self-assessment and self-adjustment, so that they can manage and control their own learning.

Helping pupils become their own best assessors

To become independent learners, students must develop a sophisticated combination of skills, attitudes and dispositions. Students become productive learners when they see that the results of their work are part of critical and constructive decision making. They need to learn to reflect on their own learning, to review their experiences of learning (What made sense and what didn't? How does this fit with what I already know, or think I know?) and to apply what they have learned to their future learning.

Self-monitoring and self-regulation are complex and difficult skills that do not develop quickly or spontaneously. Teachers have responsibility for fostering and cultivating these skills. The rest of this chapter is concerned with how teachers can foster the development of self-assessment and self-regulation in pupils.

Habits of mind for self-regulated thinking

A number of writers have referred to the 'habits of mind' that creative, critical and self-regulated thinkers use and that students (and many adults, for that matter) need to develop. These habits are ways of thinking that will enable them to learn on their own, whatever they want or need to know at any point in their lives (Marzano *et al.*, 1993).

When people succeed or fail, they can explain their success or failure to themselves in various ways: effort, ability, mood, knowledge, luck, help, interest, clarity of instructions, unfair policies and so on. Some of these are controllable, others are not. Attribution theory makes clear that to the extent that successes and failures are explained by (attributed to) controllable factors, adaptive motivational tendencies will follow (Weiner, 2000). Self-assessment is the mechanism by which learners assign attributions to particular outcomes and the teacher's role is to help pupils learn how to shift their attributions away from uncontrollable explanations (like ability) to controllable ones (like effort). A student who explains a poor result in a maths test by appealing to a lack of ability will be more likely to repeat the same behaviour pattern and meet with the same result on a future occasion than one who attributes the outcome to having not studied the correct material. In the latter example, the subsequent behaviour pattern actually shifts so that the learner asks him or herself the regulatory question 'Am I focusing on the right material?' at the outset.

Several authors have identified an 'inquiry habit of mind' as an essential component of profitable learning for individuals and groups (Newmann, 1996; Costa and Kallick, 2000; Earl and Lee, 2000; Katz *et al.*, 2002). If pupils are going to develop these 'habits of mind' and become inquiry-minded, they need to experience continuous, genuine success. They need to feel as if they are in an environment where it is safe to take chances and where feedback and support are readily available and challenging. This does not mean the absence of failure. It means using their habits of mind to identify misconceptions and inaccuracies and work with them towards a more complete and coherent understanding. Teachers have the responsibility of creating environments for pupils to become confident, competent self-assessors who monitor their own learning.

Lots of examples of 'what good work looks like'

As Sadler (1989) suggested, pupils' ideas of quality can approach those of the teacher if they have good exemplification and support; this is what he refers to as 'guild knowledge'. This knowledge is a prerequisite for pupils taking responsibility for their own learning and for setting their own targets, since success is only possible if the end results are clearly delineated. Knowing what good work looks like not only increases the learner's conceptual awareness and provides reference points to strive for, but also enhances his or her metacognitive awareness of the progress of learning. With such insight and engagement pupils become more proficient in monitoring their work continuously during production whilst developing sustainable learning and self-assessment skills. They develop a repertoire of approaches such as editing and self-evaluating in addition to that of setting their own targets, since their needs become apparent as part of the procedure. If, as Sadler argued, self-assessment is essential to learning because students can only achieve a learning goal if they understand that goal and can assess what they need to do to reach it, the criteria for evaluating any learning achievements must be made transparent to students to enable them to have a clear overview both of the aims of their work and of what it means to complete it successfully.

Although curriculum guides and standards (such as the national curriculum, schemes of work and level descriptions) provide a skeleton image of the expectations for students, nothing is as powerful as multiple images of 'what it looks like when experts do it'. Not only do pupils begin to see, hear and feel the expectations for the work at hand, they become acutely aware of the variations that can occur and the legitimacy of those variations. Once learners have a sense of where they are aiming, teachers can offer many intermediate examples of the stages along the way and how experts also struggle to meet their own expectations.

Many assessment methods have the potential to encourage reflection and review. What matters in assessment as learning is that the methods allow students to consider their own learning in relation to models, exemplars, criteria, rubrics, frameworks and checklists that provide images of successful learning. When pupils contribute to developing these models, they are even more likely to internalise them and develop a concrete image of what 'good work looks like'.

Real involvement and responsibility

When teachers work to involve pupils and to promote their independence, they are really teaching pupils to be responsible for their own learning and giving them the tools to undertake it wisely and well (Stiggins, 2001). How else are they likely to develop the self-regulatory skills that are the hallmark of experts? It isn't likely, however, that pupils will become competent, realistic self-evaluators on their own. They need to be taught skills of self-assessment, have routine and challenging opportunities to practise and develop internal feedback or self-monitoring mechanisms to validate and to call into question their own judgements. They compare their progress towards an achievement goal and create an internal feedback loop for learning. The more control and choice that students have in thinking about their learning, the less likely they are to attribute their understanding (or lack of understanding) to external factors like teachers or subject matter. Instead, they become more responsible for their learning and have increased self-efficacy and resilience. For pupils to become independent learners they need to develop a complicated combination of skills, attitudes and dispositions in order to set goals, organise their thinking, self-monitor and self-correct. Each of these skills can be learned by engaging pupils in these activities and helping them change their learning plans based on what they learn, over and over again during their years in school.

Targeted feedback

Learning is enhanced when pupils see the effects of what they have tried, and can envision alternative strategies to understand the material. Although assessment as learning is designed to develop independent learning, pupils cannot accomplish it without the guidance and direction that comes from detailed and relevant descriptive feedback from teachers to help them identify their learning needs and to develop autonomy and competence (Gipps et al., 2000; Clarke, 2003). Students need feedback not just about the status of their learning but also about the degree to which they know when, where and how to use the knowledge they are learning (Bransford et al., 1999). Effective feedback challenges ideas, introduces additional information, offers alternative interpretations and creates conditions for self-reflection and the review of ideas. Pupils can apply these approaches for themselves to monitor their own learning, think about where they feel secure in their learning and where they feel confused or uncertain, and decide on a learning plan. In so doing pupils are encouraged to focus their attention on the task rather than on getting the answer right, and they develop ideas for adjusting, rethinking and articulating their understanding.

Discussion, challenge and reflection

As Vygotsky (1978) argued, the capacity to learn from others is fundamental to human intelligence. With help from someone more knowledgeable or skilled, the learner is able to achieve more than she or he could achieve alone. Ideas are not transported 'ready-made' into students' minds. Instead, as the Jojo story showed, new ideas emerge through careful consideration and reasoned analysis, and just as important through interaction with new ideas from the physical and social worlds. Learning is not private and it isn't silent. It may happen in individual minds but it is constantly connected to the world outside and the people in that world. Peers and parents can be strong advocates and contributors to this process, not as judges, meeting out marks or favours, but as participants in the process of analysis, comparison, rethinking and reinforcing that makes up learning. Learning is a social activity. Teachers, peers and parents, when they understand their role, and the situation is structured to support the process, can be key players as learners grapple with 'what they believe to be true' in relation to the views, perspectives and challenges of others.

Practice, practice, practice

Independence in monitoring learning isn't something that just occurs. It doesn't happen immediately and there may be setbacks along the way. Even those with natural talent require a great deal of practice in order to develop their expertise. But practice is more than repetitive drills. Modern theories of learning and transfer retain the emphasis on practice, but they specify the kinds of practice that are important, and take learner characteristics (for example, existing knowledge and strategies) into account. Learning and transfer is most effective when people engage in 'deliberate practice' that includes active monitoring of their learning experiences (Bransford *et al.*, 1999). When teachers involve pupils and promote independence they are making their students responsible for their own learning and giving them the tools to undertake it wisely and well, by allowing them to experiment with new ideas, try them on, see how they fit, struggle with the misfits and come to grips with them. Effective problem solvers monitor their own mental progress as they plan for, execute and reflect on a learning task, and learners need opportunities to talk aloud overtly about what is going on inside their heads. This requires many opportunities to practise, reflect, challenge and try again.

An environment of emotional safety

Becoming independent and responsible learners who embrace assessment as a positive part of the process is not something that comes easily. In fact, it is downright scary for many adults, let alone young people. It is no surprise that some (perhaps many) students do not wholeheartedly embrace the idea. The extent to which pupils are willing to engage in self-assessment is very much connected to their sense of self and their self-esteem. Persistence depends on expectations of success, even if it is not immediate. However, pupils who have had a history of, or fear, failure will adopt techniques to protect themselves, even if it means avoiding opportunities for learning. Pupils who define themselves by their ability are often dependent on high grades as a visible symbol of their worth, and find the challenge of moving away from their positions of confidence rather like a free fall into the unknown. It isn't enough to have a few safe moments or episodes of learning. These need to be the norm. Through detailed case studies of individual children throughout their primary schooling, Pollard and Filer (1999) demonstrate how these pupils continuously shaped their identities and actively evolved as they moved from one classroom context to the next. What this means is that each child's sense of self as a pupil can be enhanced or threatened by changes over time in their relationships, structural position in the classroom and relative success or failure. Their sense of self was particularly affected by their teachers' expectations, learning and teaching strategies, classroom organisation and criteria for evaluation.

If students are going to feel at ease with self-monitoring and self-regulation, they need to be comfortable with identifying different possibilities; they need to learn to look for misconceptions and inaccuracies in their own thinking and work towards a more complete and coherent understanding. Students (both those who have been successful – in a system that rewards safe answers – and those who are accustomed to failure) are often unwilling to confront challenges and take the risks associated with making their thinking visible. Teachers have the responsibility for creating environments in which students can become confident, competent self-assessors by providing emotional security and genuine opportunities for involvement, independence and responsibility.

Images and points for reflection

Changing assessment to capitalise on its power to enhance learning can be a fundamental shift in the preconceptions that teachers have about assessment – about what it is for, how it is connected to learning and how it works. In fact, shifting to routines in the classroom where assessment is used to help pupils monitor and regulate their own learning requires that teachers draw on their personal metacognitive skills and engage in a process of rethinking their assessment and teaching practices. Teachers, like students, may need help, feedback and reflection so that they can try out and adapt their new acquired skills and knowledge in new environments. And they need images of how assessment can contribute to student reflection and self-regulation. We have included three examples to stimulate thinking about what using assessment for self-monitoring and self-regulation might look like, and as a starting point for creating others.

Image 1 – primary mathematics

A primary teacher has been teaching the concept of two-digit addition with regrouping. She uses a worksheet that includes a range of items (such as single digit additions without regrouping, single digit with regrouping, double digit additions with and without regrouping, and tricky additions). These items enable her to become an investigator, making inferences and establishing hypotheses about what different pupils understand and what is still unclear or even inaccurate in their conceptions. After she analyses the pupils' work, she conducts a 'think aloud' with the class for each of the items, in which she models her thinking as she attempts each question. In this way she provides them with insights about the correct approach as well as indicating the kinds of misconceptions and errors that might creep into someone's thinking. Finally, she does individual 'think alouds' with selected students, in which they tell her what they were thinking as they did particular questions (that she identified from their pattern of errors) so that she can help them see where their thinking needs some adjustment or practice. These targeted moments of reflection and rethinking on the part of individual pupils also provide information that forms the basis for the next stage in teaching and the grouping of pupils.

Points for reflection

1. What content knowledge does this teacher need to construct this assessment?
2. What predictable patterns of errors would the teacher look for in analysing the students' work?
3. How has the teacher created opportunities for individual students to see their own thinking, reflect on it and make adjustments? What other strategies might she use now that she has additional information about their thinking?

Image 2 – middle years social studies

One of the history curriculum targets for pupils in key stage 3 is 'organisation and communication'. This overarching objective includes several sub-items: recall, prioritise and select historical information; accurately select and use chronological conventions; and communicate knowledge and understanding of historical events. Within 'recall, prioritise and select historical information' alone there are five additional sub-items: organising information; using a range of sources of information; finding relevant information; sorting, classifying and sequencing information; and comparing/contrasting information. The possibility of gaps in knowledge, underdeveloped skills, misunderstandings or misconceptions and confusion for pupils is massive. If teachers are serious about assessment for learning, every assessment task (and there will be many, both formal and informal) should provide insight into different pupils' status in relation to organisation and communication of history and give pupils the reference points and the exemplars to allow them to reflect on their own thinking. Each assessment should explicitly focus on a subset of the skills, understanding, conventions, etc. that make up the overall curriculum expectation. And the teacher's job is not just to score the assignments; rather (s)he takes each assignment and, over time, constructs and continually adjusts the profile of learning and of teaching for each pupil, in order to move their learning forward in effective and efficient ways.

Points for reflection

1.   What are the likely gaps in prior knowledge, areas of difficulty, misconceptions and challenges that students are likely to exhibit in relation to organising information; using a range of sources of information; finding relevant information; sorting, classifying and sequencing information; and comparing/contrasting information?

2.   Design an assessment task for 'recall, prioritise and select historical information' that allows students to make decisions about their own knowledge and skill in relation to organising information; using a range of sources of information; finding relevant information; sorting, classifying and sequencing information; and comparing/contrasting information.

Image 3 – middle years mathematics

At the beginning of the school year, a middle school mathematics teacher uses a series of 'games' that he has devised to give him insights into his pupils' knowledge and depth of understanding of concepts in the mathematics curriculum. One of these games uses a modified pool table to help him ascertain the pupils' conceptions of algebraic relationships, either formal or intuitive. Pupils were given a graphic of a four-pocket pool table. They were told that the ball always leaves pocket A at a 45° angle, rebounds off a wall at an equal angle to that at which the wall was struck, and continues until it ends up in a pocket. Pupils counted the number of squares the ball passed through as well as the number of hits the ball made, the first and last hit being the starting and finishing pockets. They experimented with tables of various dimensions and recorded their observations on a chart (see Table 6.1).

Table 6.1 Pool table dimensions and observations

Length	Width	Number of hits	Number of squares
6	4	5	12
3	5	8	15
5	4		
3	2		
8	4		

As the pupils gathered data (with many more data combinations than we have included in the table), they began to make predictions about the number of hits, the number of squares and the destination of the ball, based on the patterns that they observed. Some moved to general statements of relationships like 'You can tell the number of hits by adding the width and the length together and dividing by their greatest common factor.' Or, 'The number of squares that the ball goes through is always the lowest common multiple of the width and the length.' Other students continued to count to reach the answers without seeing the relationships that existed.

During this task, the teacher wandered around the room observing and noting the thinking that was occurring for individual pupils. He stopped and asked questions, not about the answers that they were recording but about the process that they were using. He prompted them to think about the patterns and to take a chance at making predictions. All the while he was making notes on a pad that contained the names of the students and blank fields for writing his observations. From this information he decided how to proceed in teaching the next series of lessons and how to group the class for the various teaching elements to come. For some, the work progressed very quickly to an introduction of formal notation of an algebraic equation to symbolise the general patterns that they had identified. For others, he used a number of patterning exercises to help them see the patterns that arose and formulate them in very concrete ways. He was very conscious of the importance of moving from concrete experience and direct consciousness of the phenomenon to the more abstract representation. The pool table task gave him a window into his pupils' thinking and a starting place for planning teaching, resources, grouping, timing and pacing. When he moves on to another concept all of these are likely to change. Once again, he will need to find out what the students see, what they think and what they understood before he decides what to do.

Points for reflection

1. What mathematical content knowledge did this teacher need to have to design this task? To learn from this task?
2. What are the patterns of prior learning that he would be looking for in his students' thinking?
3. What guides would be required for the students to identify these patterns in their own thinking?

Further reading

The following resources may be useful for teachers in their study and implementation of classroom assessment with purpose in mind. This list is not exhaustive. Instead, it includes examples of books, articles, materials and web links that can be the starting point for individuals and groups to build their own personalised assessment resource compendia.

Active Learning Practice for Schools: Teaching for Understanding. Online, available at: learnweb.harvard.edu/alps/tfu/index.cfm (accessed 11 July 2007).

Airasian, P.W. (1999) *Assessment in the Classroom: a concise approach* (2nd edn), New York, NY: McGraw-Hill.

Arter, J. and Busick, K. (2001) *Practice with Student-Involved Classroom Assessment*, Portland, OR: Assessment Training Institute.

Arter, J. and McTighe, J. (2001) *Scoring Rubrics in the Classroom*, Thousand Oaks, CA: Corwin.

Association for Achievement and Improvement through Assessment. Online, available at: www.aaia.org.uk (accessed 11 July 2007).

Black, P. and Harrison, C. (2001) 'Feedback in questioning and marking: the science teacher's role in formative assessment', *School Science Review*, 82: 55–61.

Black, P., Harrison, C., Lee, C., Marshall, B. and Wiliam, D. (2003) *Assessment for Learning: putting it into practice*, Maidenhead: Open University Press.

Blythe, T., Allen, D. and Schieffelin, P.B. (1999) *Looking Together at Student Work: a companion guide to assessing student learning*, New York, NY: Teachers' College Press.

Earl, L. (2003) *Assessment as Learning: using classroom assessment to maximize student learning*, Thousand Oaks, CA: Corwin.

Gipps, C., McCallum, B. and Hargreaves, E. (2000) *What Makes a Good Primary School Teacher? Expert classroom strategies*, London: RoutledgeFalmer.

Gregory, G. and Kuzmich, L. (2004) *Data-Driven Differentiation in the Standards-Based Classroom*, Thousand Oaks, CA: Corwin.

Griffin, P., Smith, P. and Martin, L. (2003) *Profiles in English as a Second Language*, Clifton Hill, Victoria, BC: Robert Andersen and Associates.

Griffin, P., Smith, P. and Ridge, N. (2001) *The Literacy Profiles in Practice: toward authentic assessment*, Portsmouth, NH: Heinemann.

Joint Committee on Standards for Educational Evaluation (2000) *The Student Evaluation*, Kalamazoo, MI: The Evaluation Center, Western Michigan University.

Little, J.W., Gearhart, M., Curry, M. and Kafka, J. (2003) 'Looking at student work for teacher learning, teacher community, and school reform', *Phi Delta Kappan*, 85: 185–92.

National Research Council (1999) *How People Learn: bridging research and practice*, Committee on Learning Research and Educational Practice, Washington, DC: National Academy Press.

Rolheiser, C., Bower, B. and Stevahn, L. (2000) *The Portfolio Organizer: succeeding with portfolios in your classroom*, Alexandria, VA: Association for Supervision and Curriculum Development.

References

Assessment Reform Group (1999) *Assessment for Learning: beyond the black box*, Cambridge: University of Cambridge School of Education.

Black, P. and Wiliam, D. (1998a) 'Assessment and classroom learning', *Assessment in Education*, 5: 7–74.

—— (1998b) *Inside the Black Box*, London: King's College.

Bransford, J.D., Brown, A.L. and Cocking, R.R. (1999) *How People Learn: brain, mind, experience, and school*, Washington, DC: National Academy Press.

Brown, A. (1987) 'Metacognition, executive control, self-regulation, and mysterious mechanisms', in F. Weinert and R. Kluwe (eds) *Metacognition, Motivation, and Understanding*, Mahwah, NJ: Erlbaum.

Clarke, S. (2003) *Enriching Feedback in the Primary Classroom*, London: Hodder and Stoughton.

Costa, A. (2006) *Developing Minds: a resource book for teaching thinking* (3rd edn), Alexandria, VA: Association for Supervision and Curriculum Development.

Costa, A. and Kallick, B. (2000) *Activating and Engaging Habits of Mind*, Alexandria, VA: Association for Supervision and Curriculum Development.

Crooks, T. (1988) 'The impact of classroom evaluation practices on students', *Review of Educational Research*, 58: 438–81.

Delors, J., Al Mufti, I., Amagi, A., Carneiro, R., Chung, F., Geremek, B., Gorham, W., Kornhauser, A., Manley, M., Padrón Quero, M., Savané, M-A., Singh, K., Stavenhagen, R., Suhr, M.W. and Nanzhao, Z. (1996) *Learning: the treasure within*, report to UNESCO of the International Commission on Education for the twenty-first century, Paris: UNESCO.

Earl, L. (2003) *Assessment as Learning: using classroom assessment to maximize student learning*, Thousand Oaks, CA: Corwin.

Earl, L. and Katz, S. (2005) *Rethinking Assessment with Purpose in Mind*, Western and Northern Canadian Protocol for Collaboration in Education.

Earl, L. and Lee, L. (2000) 'Learning, for a change: school improvement as capacity building', *Improving Schools*, 3: 30–8.

Gipps, C., McCallum, B. and Hargreaves, E. (2000) *What Makes a Good Primary School Teacher? Expert classroom strategies*, London: RoutledgeFalmer.

Katz, S. (2000) 'Competency, epistemology and pedagogy: curriculum's holy trinity', *Curriculum Journal*, 11: 133–44.

Katz, S., Sunderland, S. and Earl, L. (2002) 'Developing an evaluation habit of mind', *Canadian Journal of Program Evaluation*, 17: 103–19.

King, P.M. and Kitchener, K.S. (1994) *Developing Reflective Judgement: understanding and prompting intellectual growth and critical thinking in adolescents and adults*, San Francisco, CA: Jossey-Bass.

Marzano, R., Pickering, D. and McTighe, J. (1993) *Assessing Student Outcomes: performance assessment using the dimensions of learning mode*, Alexandria, VA: Association for Supervision and Curriculum Development.

Newmann, F. (1996) *Authentic Achievement: restructuring schools for intellectual quality*, San Francisco, CA: Jossey-Bass.

Pollard, A. and Filer, A. (1999) *The Social World of Children's Learning*, London: Cassell.

Sadler, R. (1989) 'Formative assessment and the design of instructional systems', *Instructional Science*, 18: 119–44.

Stiggins, R. (2001) *Student-Involved Classroom Assessment*, Upper Saddle River, NJ: Merrill Prentice Hall.

Vygotsky, L.S. (1978) *Mind in Society: the development of the higher psychological processes* (originally published in 1930, Oxford University Press, New York edn), Cambridge, MA: Harvard University Press.

Weiner, B. (2000) 'Intrapersonal and interpersonal theories of motivation from an attributional perspective', *Educational Psychology Review*, 12: 1–14.

Understanding and using assessment data

Pete Dudley and Sue Swaffield

Educators and the public need to develop assessment literacy in order to examine student work and performance data of all types and to make critical sense of it.

(Earl *et al.*, 2000)

Introduction

Understanding and using assessment data is at the heart of assessment for learning, as indicated by the Assessment Reform Group's definition of AfL: 'The process of seeking and *interpreting evidence for use* by learners and their teachers to decide where the learners are in their learning, where they need to go next, and how best to get there' (ARG, 2002) (italics added). In order to interpret assessment evidence appropriately we need to understand how it was generated, its limitations and the confidence we may have in it. Then we can decide how to use the information to aid pupils' learning, by knowing more clearly what their precise needs are, what will engage them in their learning and how their learning can be supported within and beyond the classroom. This process has now also become known as 'personalising learning and teaching', defined by the 'Teaching and learning in 2020 review group' as '... taking a highly structured and responsive approach to each child's and young person's learning' (DfES, 2006a: 6).

Using assessment data is not something that can be considered in isolation, and is integral to many other chapters in this volume. 'Assessment data' is often thought of as numbers, figures or grades derived from tests and other forms of 'formal' assessment, and certainly they feature more in this chapter than in others. However, we take a broad view of data including pupils' oral responses and their written work.

In this chapter we examine some key issues, look at ways in which teachers and school leaders use data, consider the analysis of performance data, discuss the use of data for personalising learning and teaching, and conclude with some principles to guide practice. Strictly speaking the word 'data' is the plural form of datum, but for ease of expression and following conventions of everyday usage we treat it as singular.

Key issues

Validity and reliability

Validity and reliability are hugely important issues, dealing as they do with the confidence we can have in assessment and the use that is made of the outcomes. These issues are dealt with in more detail in other chapters in this volume by Dylan Wiliam and Wynne Harlen, but certain points should be highlighted here.

The traditional view of validity is whether an assessment assesses what it claims to assess, and although the concept has now become more encompassing (see Wiliam's chapter), this idea remains a good starting point. National curriculum assessment as it has evolved is not actually assessment of the national curriculum, but only a subset of the curriculum, largely focusing on parts of English, mathematics and science that are assessed through tests. It does not assess other important aspects of schooling such as personal, social and health education, citizenship, interpersonal skills, emotional intelligence, thinking skills or learning dispositions. Nor are the five outcomes of 'Every Child Matters' tested. Part of the reason is that these other aspects are more difficult to assess, at least in tests, and herein lies a danger known as the Macnamara fallacy, tellingly summarized by Charles Handy:

> The first step is to measure whatever can be easily measured. This is OK as far as it goes. The second step is to disregard that which can't easily be measured or to give it an arbitrary quantitative value. This is artificial and misleading. The third step is to presume that what can't be measured easily really isn't important. This is blindness. The fourth step is to say that what can't be easily measured really doesn't exist. This is suicide.
>
> (Handy, 1994: 219)

Things that it is possible to measure are chosen as indicators of something wider, unfortunately often with the consequence known as Goodhart's law, which has been summarized as 'performance indicators lose their usefulness when used as objects of policy' (Wiliam, 2001a: 60). This is because when a measure is used as an indicator of a system, so much attention can be placed on raising the scores on that particular measure that other aspects are neglected and overall performance may decline even though one set of scores increases.

However, it is also important to note that schools in which pupils consistently make very good progress as measured through these tests (see below and DfES, 2007a), tend to have a broad, balanced and creative curriculum. In a sense then the parts of the curriculum that are subject to national tests may be viewed as proxy indicators for wider aspects of learning and school performance. Later in this chapter we will look at progress being made in improving the consistency and quality of teacher assessments.

Whereas validity is concerned with what we measure and what it means, reliability is concerned with the accuracy of our measurement. It is generally assumed that assessments made under test conditions are more reliable than those made by teachers during their normal interactions with students. However, it is worth noting that in relation to national curriculum tests Dylan Wiliam has estimated that:

> the proportion of students getting a level higher or lower than they should have got, due to the unreliability of the test, is at least 30% at key stage 2 and may be as high as 40% at key stage 3.
>
> (Wiliam, 2001b: 11)

Standardized test scores are often used because they seem to give a more precise measurement and often this is related to the age (in years and months) of the pupil. These scores are produced using statistical predictions however. If a child gets a standardized score of 110 in any test this means in reality that there is a 90 per cent probability that they would have scored between 102 and 118. Few people are aware of this wide margin of error.

These imprecisions do not matter for the system as a whole or when considering large groups of students because the mis-classifications will even themselves out, but it may make a difference for small groups of pupils and perhaps have more serious consequences for individuals. The case for trusting teachers' judgements is made by Wynne Harlen in her chapter in this volume, in which she also points out that the need for high reliability depends upon the use made of the result.

The high priority currently given to measurement and quantification in the English school system sits within a policy framework of public service agreements, targets and high stakes accountability. It is beyond the scope of this chapter to go into these issues in any depth, but it is important to be aware of the political and cultural backdrop to the current system in England.

Bases of comparison

All assessment involves making judgements in relation to something. For example, we may assess a piece of work by comparing it with that of other pupils, or with success criteria, or with work of a similar nature previously produced by the same pupil. In practice we tend to do all of these things, although we may not always be conscious of the approach we are using. The basis of comparison that is used affects the kind of data that is produced, the kinds of inferences that can be made and their use. The technical terms for each of the three kinds of referencing systems are norm, criterion and ipsative referencing.

Norm referencing is concerned with comparing a pupil with other pupils, or with 'the average' pupil. It enables you to say how well a particular child is doing in relation to others in the class, or any other group for whom the information is available. These judgements were once typically expressed in terms of 'fifth in the class' (or whatever), reflecting individual ranking. Nowadays phrases such as 'in the top 20 per cent', 'in the second set', 'performing as expected for year 3' or 'below average', are more common. The beliefs and values behind these statements are quite closely related to concepts of fixed intelligence and ability. Norm-referenced assessment encourages labelling, and since there is very little that an individual can do to change his or her position in relation to others (we can change our own performance but not that of everyone else) it can have a detrimental influence on motivation and self-esteem. The results of norm-referenced assessment do not say anything about what a pupil can or cannot actually do, and so are not helpful in taking learning forward.

With criterion referencing the judgement is made against pre-specified criteria, irrespective of the performance of other pupils. Criterion-referenced assessments can help pinpoint what a learner knows, understands or can do, as well as any gaps or misunderstandings. If the criteria used for a particular piece of work have been derived from a set curriculum or scheme of work the next steps are often clearly indicated – redressing any misconceptions, consolidating the learning or moving on to other objectives. One of the issues with criterion-referenced assessment is how precisely and tightly focused the criteria should be. High specificity can be helpful in planning teaching, guiding learning and making assessments, but it can also result in very prescriptive learning experiences, antithetical to unanticipated opportunities and spontaneity. It can also result in teaching, learning and assessment being tightly focused on seemingly unrelated items, as well as making the whole process difficult to manage. As is so often the case there is no single answer since different degrees of detail are appropriate in different circumstances, and have varied implications. Narrowly focused criteria can be very helpful to both learner and teacher if the focus is on developing skills or detailed understanding, but when applying a range of skills to an extended piece of work the criteria need to be wider. A very broad expression of criteria can be found in the national curriculum level descriptions, designed to summarize learning that may have taken two years to master. Assessment judgements that are made against criteria as all encompassing as these are very broad brush, giving indications of general performance but providing no detail. In balancing overall strengths and weaknesses a teacher could quite correctly judge two pupils with different profiles of performance to be at the same level. Similarly, two students could score exactly the same total marks in a test, but vary considerably in their grasp of the aspects tested. So to understand a criterion-referenced assessment we must be aware of the specificity of the criteria used, and the manner in which the judgement was made (for example, as 'best-fit', or 'has attained all parts'). It really is not as simple as assuming that because a pupil has been judged to be level 4 in maths, say, that he or she has a firm grasp of *everything* that constitutes level 4, and that the appropriate next step is work deemed to be 'level 5'. There may still be knowledge, skills or understanding at level 4 that need to be taught or consolidated.

The third kind of referencing is 'ipsative', a word not in common use even though the concept is one we all use every day. Derived from the Latin 'ipse' meaning self, this form of assessment involves judgements in relation to the particular pupil's previous performance. Ipsative referencing allows us to tailor our judgements and comments to the individual, recognizing a piece of work as a major achievement for one pupil, whilst at the same time responding in quite a different way if presented with exactly the same standard of work from another pupil. In order to make judgements in this way we need to have detailed knowledge of the pupil's previous performance, but this then enables us to individualize our comments and plan appropriate next steps. Pupils too can judge how well their work is developing, feel a sense of satisfaction from the improvement and be recognized for their progress irrespective of general expectations or what others have done. This is important for everyone, and perhaps particularly for those at either end of the attainment range.

These notions of different bases for comparison help us distinguish between two words that are often used synonymously, but actually have usefully different meanings. When we talk about someone's *achievement* there is an implication of effort involved. Achievement is ipsative referenced: an achievement for one person may not be for another. *Attainment*, on the other hand, relates to criterion referencing. An attainment may or may not be an achievement for me, depending on my previous attainment and the effort involved. As an example, swimming a mile may be a massive achievement for one person, but something that another does every morning with ease. In both cases though what is attained, swimming a mile, is the same. Whilst often used interchangeably the subtle differences between attainment and achievement can be very revealing. Both concepts are important.

We have presented the three forms of referencing, norm, criterion and ipsative, as though they are distinct, but in practice they interrelate. Notions of norm referencing often underlie criterion referencing. For example, national curriculum criteria relate to expected attainment for most or 'average' pupils of a certain age.

How schools are using data

Assessment data can be used in many ways, and in 2005 the National Foundation for Educational Research (NfER) carried out a study for the DfES to identify how schools in England were using data (Kirkup *et al.*, 2005). It was found that in all types of schools data was perceived to promote teaching and learning by facilitating (Kirkup *et al.*, 2005: 1):

- more effective allocation of staff and resources
- performance management
- monitoring the effectiveness of initiatives and strategies
- evidence-based discussions with the Office for Standards in Education (OFSTED), local education authorities (LEAs), governors, etc.
- challenging expectations of staff, pupils, parents, among others
- transitions and transfers – particularly transitions between key stages within schools
- identification of pupils' achievements and setting of targets.

The items on this list emphasize school level uses rather than those that directly affect pupils, although other summary lists of uses within the report put pupils more directly and obviously in the picture. For example, reported uses for data were to:

- track pupil progress
- set targets
- identify underachieving pupils for further support
- inform teaching and learning and strategic planning
- inform the setting and grouping of pupils (particularly in secondary schools)
- monitor the effectiveness of staff and initiatives
- provide reports to parents (notably in special schools)
- highlight specific weaknesses for individual pupils
- identify weaknesses in topics for the class as a whole
- inform accurate curricular targets for individual pupils
- provide evidence to support decisions as to where to focus resources and teaching.

Where data analysis highlighted issues these were often addressed by providing additional support and making changes to the teaching programme. The report stressed that the important thing is the use to which data is put and that 'data only becomes effective if it stimulates questions about the actual learning that is taking place and how it can be developed further' (Kirkup *et al.*, 2005: 1). Schools in the study reported that meaningful dialogue among staff was important for the effective use of data.

Another study looked at 20 schools with 'outstanding rates of progression in key stage 2' (DfES, 2007a). The specific criterion for inclusion in the study was that 90 per cent or more of their pupils who were at level 2 at key stage 1 progressed to level 4 at key stage 2. Perhaps not surprisingly considering that the schools' selection was based on national curriculum attainment, the interpretation and use of assessment data figured prominently in the common characteristics of these schools. 'The single most effective thing all the schools were doing was to track the progress of their pupils regularly, vigorously and individually' (DfES, 2007a: 6). This tracking gave very detailed information about each child's performance, aptitudes, strengths and learning needs. Senior staff were directly involved with the monitoring of pupils' progress, an activity that was described as being 'hands-on' and concerned with tracking pupils rather than marks. It went beyond the analysis of numbers to the regular scrutiny of pupils' work, and keeping close tabs on individuals. All the schools had long- and medium-term curriculum plans in place that supported progression throughout the school, and 'a strong emphasis is placed on using summative assessment at the end of the school year to inform planning for the following year' (DfES, 2007a: 20). Tried and tested plans were used as a starting point, and then amended and adapted to suit the needs of children, and to ensure that each cohort made optimum progress from year to year. School self-evaluation identified areas of the curriculum that were not being addressed as well as others, and then the whole staff shared responsibility for improvement. Pupils had personal targets that were specific and challenging, and were followed up. In lessons there was a strong focus on the use of questioning to identify pupils' understanding. This revealed information that was then used to plan the next steps in teaching and learning. The report states that 'If a child fails to make the required progress, it is never deemed to be his/her fault, rather teachers look to themselves and to their teaching' (DfES, 2007a: 25).

Both these studies paint pictures of schools where staff are very skilled at, and committed to, regularly analysing and using national curriculum attainment and progress data to inform their planning and teaching. A report of two earlier similar surveys (Ashby and Sainsbury, 2001) found that by 2000 a number of schools had clear strategies for making full use of test information. By 2008 it is undoubtedly the case that the vast majority of schools are doing so with ever increasing sophistication. However, with this practice now so widespread and embedded, it is well worth repeating the note of caution that Ashby and Sainsbury sounded in their conclusion in 2001. 'Attention to test results could go beyond an optimum level, with the result that the curriculum becomes too focused upon test preparation, to the detriment of pupils and staff' (Ashby and Sainsbury, 2001: 23–4).

With this note of caution ringing in our ears, let us turn to look at data analysis in more detail.

The analysis of performance data

Since the introduction of national curriculum assessment vast quantities of test and teacher assessment data have been generated. For each pupil these include results in different subjects (especially English, maths and science), in different aspects of a subject (for example reading and writing in English) and over time (at the end of each key stage, at the end of each year and at regular points during the year). Individual pupil results can be aggregated to provide data relating to groups, classes, cohorts, key stages, schools, local authorities and the country as a whole. The data can be analysed in four main ways:

1. for raw scores, allowing us to report results for an individual or give the percentage of a year group achieving level 4 in maths for example;

2. to make comparisons, between different groups or against expectations;

3. to look backwards to reveal trends and see what progress has been made ('value added' or 'conversion' data);

4. to look ahead, to set targets and make projections about future performance.

Additional details about background characteristics such as pupils' ethnic group, first language and mobility enable data to be put in context, and for more meaningful comparisons to be made among broadly similar individuals and groups. Being able to match data to individuals over time, particularly when pupils move schools, and ensuring that datasets are as up-to-date and accurate as possible, enhance the confidence we can have in the data and therefore the inferences we draw. IT systems and powerful software (for example those used by the interactive RAISEonline report for each school, and the Fischer Family Trust) increase the sophistication of possible analyses.

The analysis and interpretation of performance data are key elements in school self-evaluation and inspection, and are central to the work of school improvement partners whose accreditation depends upon their competence in this area. Ofsted provides guidance for inspectors on the use of school performance data (Ofsted, 2006) and since inspection is now so interlinked with school self-evaluation this guidance is highly pertinent for teachers and school leaders too. Inspectors are required to make separate judgements about standards and progress and to do so they look at a lot of pupil performance data, analysed in different ways.

Headlines scores such as the percentage of pupils reaching level 4 and above at key stage 2 give an initial impression about standards, while average point scores take into account performance across the whole attainment range. At key stage 4 particularly, headline results can vary depending on the rubric for which subjects are included in the calculation. Similarities and differences between subjects and key stages are looked at, and a school's results are compared with national expectations and national results. Trends over time are examined and compared with national scores to see if standards in the school are improving, declining or fluctuating. Judgements about standards are made in relation to performance nationally and so are norm referenced.

Many judgements about progress are made in relation to what would be expected, given the background characteristics of the pupils and their starting points. Progress judged in this way is often referred to as 'value added', in other words the improvement from a given starting point, and put in the context of factors that could be expected to affect progress – contextual value added (CVA). Early approaches to putting results in context used a very limited range of factors, particularly free school meals and special needs. Current calculations of CVA take account of factors such as previous attainment, gender, mobility, learning difficulties and disabilities, ethnicity, whether English is the first language, postcode income deprivation index, care status and eligibility for free school meals. However, even this array does not consider other factors that affect performance such as support for homework or illness. There is much debate around contextual factors, a discussion that is particularly pertinent in relation to special educational needs (SEN). Pupils who are on the SEN register and receiving 'school action' in one school might have made good progress in another school without this intervention, because the teachers differentiate more successfully in their ordinary lessons and children do not fall behind. Many people now argue that a school can reduce the numbers of children in need of formal SEN support by making sure teaching meets individual needs more effectively, and by intervening quickly if pupils do fall behind. The reasoning continues that SEN should not be treated as a context factor that is beyond the school's control, and to do so rewards poor teaching. Nevertheless, some schools admit a much greater proportion of pupils with learning difficulties than others, reflecting different catchment areas and admissions policies, and this differentially affects measures of performance.

Important caveats

The national curriculum and the frameworks used for assessment and recording are predicated on a hierarchical, ladder-like model of progression. Advancement is seen as the next step on a linear, predetermined route. Whilst this reflects the idea of learning as building on prior knowledge and understanding, it precludes notions of learning as going deeper or broader (similar to Margaret Carr's ideas of wider, deeper and longer learning stories (Carr, 2001)) and suggests that 'revisiting' something entails a backward, even if necessary, step. Nor does national curriculum assessment, which is the dominant focus of this chapter, acknowledge progress as developments in participation in communities of learners as described by Jean Lave and Étienne Wenger (1991) or Barbara Rogoff (1997).

The great mass of national curriculum assessment data and powerful software make it possible to produce pages upon pages of figures, which can be extremely seductive. However, we must never forget that numbers are approximate representations of a few aspects of pupils' performance. Many decisions have been made along the way to arrive at the figures, but these decisions and therefore the provisional nature of the results are often forgotten. Clear marking procedures and moderation are helpful, but as noted above, the reliability of assessment data must always be kept in mind. CVA scores depend upon the particular factors included and how these are judged, for example the method used to determine the percentage of pupils eligible for free school meals. Where group sizes are small, just one or two pupils can make a big difference to overall school percentage figures. Cut-off points have to be determined in order to create grade boundaries, the difference between one grade and another is just one mark, and a single grade can encompass a wide range of marks. New measures, for example from the foundation stage profile (for younger children) and P-scales (for pupils recognized as having a specific learning difficulty or disability), have been introduced over time, adding to the complexity.

The data used in school level analyses relates only to a narrow focus of learning – some aspects (excluding for example speaking and listening) of two dominant subjects (English and maths) of the national curriculum, which is itself only part of what pupils learn in schools. So performance data needs to be treated with caution, and as much other information taken into account as possible. Nevertheless, it does relate to important aspects of what schools do and what pupils learn and, whilst heeding the caveats, assessment data can be extremely helpful in informing teaching and learning.

Using assessment data to personalise learning and teaching

Data and technology together can contribute to knowing whether a pupil is achieving in line with expectations. Sophisticated systems for describing, recording and tracking pupil progress over a school career make it increasingly possible to identify learning needs and the steps that can support good progress. Personalising learning, albeit a developing notion, entails using approaches that enable children to make good progress whatever their needs and motivations. It is based on teachers using their knowledge of the child, the curriculum and what progress looks like, combined with assessment and progress data. This includes the longer-term formative use of summative assessment data, as well as the absolutely critical everyday classroom practice of assessment for learning.

Formative use of summative data to support progress

In addition to the end of key stage tests, many schools use regular teacher assessment, end of unit tests and optional national curriculum tests to see how children are progressing. The data from these assessments can identify areas that a number of children have not grasped, and groups of children who may need to revisit and consolidate their learning. Question level analysis of tests may also reveal areas of the curriculum that have not been taught effectively or have been missed completely. Most schools will use this information to revise their teaching plans and approaches and/or to create new pupil groupings.

A comparison of pupils' attainment at the end of successive key stages reveals different patterns of progress and the wide range of levels awarded to pupils who at one time were assessed as being at the same level. Charts for each local authority are now being compiled annually to show the percentage of pupils making different rates of progress in national curriculum levels between the ends of key stage 2 and 3. Similar analysis at school or group level could help teachers identify and tackle underachievement and unacceptable within-school variation.

The RaiseOnline website publishes 'chances' graphs, showing the percentage of pupils reaching a particular goal (for example level 4 at key stage 2, or 5+ A*–C GCSE including English and mathematics) based on their previous attainment. Teachers have frequently found that many pupils, especially boys, are surprised by the information and motivated to try harder because they see that it is genuinely possible to thwart accepted predictions of progress. These graphs are often read as 'there is a 25 per cent chance that ...', but the language of 'chance' is ambiguous and perhaps unfortunate. Yes, all pupils do have 'a chance' of attaining a particular goal no matter what their previous attainment, even though only a relatively few pupils demonstrate more extreme patterns of progress. However, it is not 'by chance' that some make exceptional progress, or that others make no progress at all or even regress. It is not a lottery. Great improvements in attainment are possible, but they depend upon what pupils and teachers do, not luck.

Important lessons can be learnt by looking at data retrospectively, but this often only benefits succeeding cohorts of pupils. It is better to track progress, or the lack of it, as it occurs so that teaching can be adjusted and interventions put in place to benefit current pupils. Keys to this are clear notions of progression, and the day-to-day use of assessment data in all its forms. Until recently national curriculum level descriptions have been the only unit of progress to be illustrated with examples of work. Level descriptions are designed for a child to work through over two years and as such are not helpful measures for supporting pupils' progress from week to week or even term to term.

However, there is now a growing national resource exemplifying pupil progress, showing a range of pathways that pupils may take as they work at and through different stages of a national curriculum level (DfES, 2006b, 2007b). These examples have been found in pilots conducted by the Qualification and Curriculum Authority (QCA) and the national strategies to make a considerable difference to teachers' understanding of what counts as progress in a particular curriculum area. This work is now appearing as part of the national strategies primary and secondary materials. It has led to much better pitching of the next steps in learning because the teachers know more about progression in the subject area and have more detailed knowledge about where their children are against national standards. They know what good progress in the national curriculum looks like, how their children are doing and can plan better for them.

Tracking pupils' progress

Where schools have good teacher assessment processes they use termly tracking data to inform adjustments to the plans for each class and for specific pupils. The positive impact of such systems on pupil attainment was referred to above in relation to schools in the 'making great progress' study (DfES, 2007a). Pupil tracking goes hand in hand with the use of targets for groups or individuals. These help to raise expectations and give pupils and teachers a clear sense of what their goals are and a measure against which to assess. The national strategies have published 'layered targets' (that is whole school curriculum targets 'layered' to give appropriate targets for each year group) for use in the foundation stage, and key stages 1 and 2.

It is useful occasionally to take an overview of a class or group's attainment and progress in a particular curriculum area. This can be managed by concentrating on just a few features related to recent learning intentions and choosing a representative sample of pupils (QCA, 2003). Judgements can be recorded systematically in an adaptation of the traditional 'mark book'. Analysis focuses on patterns not exceptions, and the conclusions used to inform teaching. A detailed analysis of one child's work can be illuminative but it is important to be clear of the purpose of the exercise and, as with all assessment, to use the findings. A pupil tracking tool for key stages 1 and 2 can be found on the Primary Framework website (the URL is given in further reading below).

Planning for and keeping track of pupil progress should not rely on statistical data alone. Concepts maps are one of a number of possible alternative approaches. These are relational diagrams that can be used in many contexts, for example to show the elements and working of the respiratory system. Some teachers ask children to draw a concept map before beginning a new topic to reveal the extent of their current understanding. Teachers then amend plans and design activities to build on the pupils' interests and knowledge and address identified needs. As they work on a topic teacher and pupils refer to the concept maps, adding and revising as they learn. In this way concept maps act as an initial diagnostic exercise, an overview and plan of the topic, a summary of learning and a record of progress.

Other qualitative approaches to assessing and recording learning use narrative, photos, exemplars and commentary, as developed in New Zealand in the form of 'learning stories' (see Margaret Carr's and Mary-Jane Drummond's chapters in this volume, and Carr, 2001), in Italy in Reggio Emilia (Rinaldi, 2006) and around the world in the form of portfolios (Klenowski, 2002). The joy of these approaches is that they are part of the learning process, involve pupils and others as well as teachers, and celebrate and share achievement. Not many schools in England have adopted or developed these approaches to any great extent, although elements of them can be found in some classrooms, and there are considerable similarities with assessment for learning practices.

Involving pupils through assessment for learning

Assessment for learning (AfL) has the potential to raise standards (Black and Wiliam, 1998) at the same time as improving learning, relationships and the culture of the classroom. Other chapters in this volume provide more detail of its practice and effects. In recent years AfL has been championed by policy makers as well as researchers and practitioners, and has been made a key component of personalising learning and the national strategies (DfES, 2006a). AfL involves pupils in learning as active participants and constructors of understanding, and does not view them as passive recipients of information. Pupils are encouraged to assess their attainments and achievements and to decide what steps to take next, as well to feed back on each other's work. Pupils' self-assessments provide valuable information for teachers to use in adjusting lessons and revising teaching plans. A number of teachers ask students to use devices such as 'traffic light' cards, smiley faces or 'thumbs up, thumbs down' to indicate their feelings as the lesson progresses. Teachers then adjust the lesson according to whether, for example pupils are feeling confident or not understanding. Pupils' comments written in their books are data to inform future lessons.

Conclusion

In this chapter we have advocated the use of assessment data to improve learning, stressing the complexity of the issues and the importance of criticality. We have had to choose which aspects to elaborate and by necessity have given only cursory mention of others, for example school self-evaluation and the use of data to evaluate teaching strategies. Whatever the particular focus, it is useful to have principles to guide the practice of using assessment data. The Association for Improvement and Achievement through Assessment (AAIA) states that 'information from assessment should primarily be for the purpose of supporting day-to-day learning and teaching but over time should generate information that contributes to the school's self-evaluation processes' and 'all members of staff have a responsibility for assessment and should be involved in the development of practice across the school and the interpretation and use of the information generated' (AAIA, 2006: 2). These principles are expanded as follows:

Pupil progress will be supported effectively when we:

- Recognize and use the full range of information, including pupils' work, informal notes, prior and current attainment and value added data from national, local and school sources;
- Use the curriculum objectives in medium-term planning to track and monitor pupils' progress in the short to medium-term, using national curriculum levels, sub-levels and points derived from these to track progress in the longer-term;
- Use information from previous teachers to inform planning;
- Limit the quantity of information and evidence and concentrate on quality;
- Engage pupils in reviewing and recording their own progress, using evidence from their learning to help them recognize their achievements and identify their next steps;
- Use assessment information with all staff within a school/department/ key stage so that all have an understanding of the school's data and use it to evaluate learning and teaching and to support target setting;
- Use information and evidence to share and develop our understanding of levels of attainment;
- Pass on data and information which are clear and which other people find useful.

(AAIA, 2006: 6)

Points for reflection

1. Review your use of data against the principles and guidance. To what extent are you and your school using data appropriately to support pupil progress? What changes should you make?

2. What data do you have, or could be generated, about attainment and achievement in valued areas of learning other than the national curriculum, for example learning dispositions or 'Every Child Matters' outcomes?

3. At the Olympic Games different referencing systems are used for deciding who initially qualifies for an event, who is awarded a medal, whether any records have been broken and whether a competitor has improved his or her personal best. Which basis of comparison is used in each situation? Which outcome is most highly celebrated? What alternatives can you envisage? What similarities are there with pupils' assessment in school?

Further reading

Black, P. (1998) *Testing: Friend or Foe? Theory and practice of assessment and testing*, London: Falmer Press.

Gipps, C. (1994) *Beyond Testing: towards a theory of educational assessment*, London: Falmer Press.

Gipps, C. and Murphy, P. (1994) *A Fair Test? Assessment, achievement and equity*, Buckingham: Open University Press.

Stobart, G. and Gipps, C. (1997) *Assessment: a teacher's guide to the issues* (2nd edn), London: Hodder and Stoughton.

Swaffield, S. and Dudley, P. (2003) *Assessment Literacy for Wise Decisions* (2nd edn), London: Association of Teachers and Lecturers.

Wiliam, D. (2000) 'The meanings and consequences of educational assessments', *Critical Quarterly*, 42: 105–27.

The National College for School Leadership devotes part of its site to the use of data, and includes a glossary and several online learning modules. Online, available at: www.ncsl.org.uk/managing_your_school/use-of-data (accessed 27 May 2007).

The Primary Framework website of the National Strategies and the DCSF Standards sites are continually being updated with material to support teachers in using assessment data for pupil learning. From January 2008 the Primary Framework will contain a new AfL area. Online, available at: www.standards.dfes.gov.uk/primaryframeworks/ and www.standards.dfes.gov.uk/secondary/keystage3/ (accessed 10 July 2007).

References

AAIA (2006) *Using Assessment for Enhancing Learning – a practical guide*. Online, available at: www.aaia.org.uk (accessed 28 May 2007).

ARG (2002a) *Assessment for Learning: 10 principles*. Online, available at: assessment-reform-group.org (accessed 28 May 2007).

Ashby, J. and Sainsbury, M. (2001) *How do Schools use National Curriculum Test Results? A survey of the use of national curriculum test results in the management and planning of the curriculum at key stages 1 and 2.* Online, available at: www.nfer.ac.uk/publications/other-publications/downloadable-reports/how-do-schools-use-national-curriculum.cfm (accessed 28 May 2007).

Black, P. and Wiliam, D. (1998) 'Assessment and classroom learning', *Assessment in Education,* 5: 7–71.

Carr, M. (2001) *Assessment in Early Childhood Settings: learning stories,* London: Paul Chapman.

DfES (2006a) *2020 Vision: report of the teaching and learning in 2020 review group* (Gilbert Report), London: DfES.

—— (2006b) *Handbook for Assessing Pupils' Progress in English: a practical guide,* London: DfES.

—— (2007a) *Making Great Progress: schools with outstanding rates of progress in key stage 2.* London: DfES.

—— (2007b) *Assessing Pupils' Progress in Mathematics at Key Stage 3: a practical guide,* London: DfES.

Earl, L., Fullan, M., Leithwood, K. and Watson, N. (2000) *Watching and Learning: OISE/UT evaluation of the implementation of the national literacy and national numeracy strategies,* Toronto: Ontario Institute for Studies in Education of the University of Toronto.

Handy, C. (1994) *The Empty Raincoat,* London: Hutchinson.

Kirkup, C., Sizmur, J., Sturman, L. and Lewis, K. (2005) *Schools' Use of Data in Teaching and Learning* (DfES Research Report 671), London: DfES.

Klenowski, V. (2002) *Developing Portfolios for Learning and Assessment: processes and principles,* London: Routledge Falmer.

Lave, J. and Wenger, É. (1991) *Situated Learning: legitimate peripheral participation,* Cambridge: Cambridge University Press.

Ofsted (2006) *Inspection Matters: issue 10 – September 2006,* London: Ofsted.

QCA (2003) *Marking: making a difference,* London: QCA.

Rinaldi, C. (2006) *In Dialogue with Reggio Emilia: listening, researching and learning,* London: Routledge.

Rogoff, B. (1997) 'Evaluating development in the process of participation: theory, methods and practice building on each other', in E. Amsel and K. Ann Renninger (eds) *Change and Development: issues of theory, method and application,* Mahwah, NJ, and London: Erlbaum.

Wiliam, D. (2001a) 'What is wrong with our educational assessments and what can be done about it?', *Education Review,* 15: 57–62.

—— (2001b) *Level Best? Levels of attainment in national curriculum assessment,* London: Association of Teachers and Lecturers.

PART III

Assessment issues

CHAPTER 8

Quality in assessment

Dylan Wiliam

One validates, not a test, but an *interpretation of data arising from a specified procedure.*

(Cronbach, 1971: 447, emphasis in original)

Introduction

Assessment is a central process in education. It is through assessment that we can find out whether students have learned what they have been taught, so that we can make appropriate adjustments to our teaching. Assessments are used to describe the achievement of students, so that decisions can be made about their suitability for particular jobs, or the kinds of educational experiences that should follow. Parents use the results of assessments to learn about the progress their children are making at school, and to make decisions about the quality of education offered in different schools. And, of course, policy makers use assessments to provide information about the quality of schools or curricula.

Ultimately, therefore, all assessments are used to support decisions – the key idea is that a decision made with the information from the assessment is better than the decision that could be made without such information. So of course the quality of the decisions will therefore depend on the quality of the assessment.

Specialists use a range of technical terms – such as reliability, dependability, generalizability, validity, fairness and bias – to describe the quality of assessments. In this chapter, we will look at these issues not from the technical standpoint, but in terms of the impact that failure to attend to these issues can have on the quality of decisions that we make.

What can we learn from assessment results?

Consider the following scene from a classroom:

> A teacher writes 40 words on the board, and tells the class that the following day, there will be a spelling test, during which each student in the class will be asked to spell 20 words chosen at random from the 40 words written on the board. The following day, as promised, the teacher gives the students a 20-word spelling test, and collects in the students' responses. One student, Anita, spells all 20 words correctly, while another, Robin, gets 10 of the 20 words correct.

What can we conclude about the spelling ability of Anita and Robin? It seems safe to conclude that Anita is a better speller than Robin – certainly on this occasion on the 20 words actually tested – and it is probably safe to conclude that Anita would have outscored Robin on any set of 20 words chosen from the 40. While both Anita and Robin might have good days and bad days, it is very unlikely that the particular set of 20 items that were chosen suited Robin particularly badly, and Anita particularly well. Indeed, by using statistics, we can place precise limits on the probability that, in reality, Robin is able to spell more of the 40 words than Anita, but was particularly unlucky in the choice of 20 that was made on the day. It turns out to be just about impossible.

What else can we conclude? If the 20 words chosen for the spelling test were chosen at random, we can reasonably conclude that, on the basis of their performance on the test, if a different set of 20 words were chosen from the test, then Anita would probably be able to get most of them right, and that Robin would probably get about half right. In other words, we can *generalize* from the particular sample of items that were chosen for the test to the items that were not chosen. This notion of generalization is essential in assessment. We are hardly ever interested in the specific items that a test tests. Almost invariably, we are interested in the generalizations we can make once we know the students' results. We want to draw conclusions about items that were not specifically tested. The important thing about this particular example is that we are able to generalize reasonably safely from the test of 20 items to the 20 items that were not tested because the sampling of the 20 items was done at random. It would not be safe to make such a generalization if the 20 were not selected at random. This might happen, for example, if the test included the 20 easiest words to spell from the list of 40 or if we discovered that the students had somehow managed to find out which 20 items were going to be tested the day before the test.

There are other kinds of generalizations we might want to make. We might want to generalize to other testing occasions – can we safely conclude that if they know how to spell these 20 words today, they will be able to do so next week? If

they can spell words correctly in a spelling test, can they [...]
writing a story? More problematically, we might want to [...]
set of 40 words that were written on the board, and draw c[...]
words, and here we run into real trouble. Anita may have [...]
test because she is a good speller in general, or she may [...]
for the test by working very hard to learn the spelling of [...]
conclusions are warranted on the basis of the results of the [...]
are not. The process of establishing which kinds of conclusions are warranted and
which are not is called *validation* and it is, quite simply, *the* central concept in
assessment.

Validity: an evolving concept[1]

The earliest definitions of validity treated it as a property of an assessment. Kelley
(1927) pointed out 80 years ago that there were two common fallacies in educational assessment. One was the assumption that two tests[2] that claimed to be
testing the same thing must in fact be testing the same thing. The other was that
two tests that claimed to be testing different things were, indeed, testing different
things. An assessment was said to be *valid* to the extent that it really did assess
what it purported to assess. Validation was therefore the process of establishing
the extent to which the assessment was indeed, assessing what it claimed to assess.

Originally, validity was established by having panels of experts looking at tests,
and giving their opinions about whether the items were individually relevant and
collectively representative. An item was relevant if the panel agreed that the item
was assessing some aspect of whatever it was that the test was meant to be testing,
and the whole test was representative if the overall balance of the items taken
together adequately covered whatever it was that the test was meant to be testing.
Because of the focus on the content of the test, this aspect of validity was called
content validity.

However, there were cases where it was not possible to validate a test by reference to its content, because the content was not well defined. Instead, tests were
validated by their predictive properties. For example, for many years almost all
LEAs in England, Wales and Northern Ireland operated two forms of secondary
school: grammar schools for the most able students, and secondary modern
schools for the remainder (the proportion of students attending grammar school
ranged from 5 per cent in some LEAs to over 30 per cent in others). The criterion for admission to a grammar school was 'the ability to benefit from a
grammar school education' – a rather circular definition. How students were to
be selected for grammar schools was left to the LEAs, and many relied on intelligence tests (usually called the '11 plus'), sometimes in conjunction with headteacher ratings.

...idity of the intelligence tests for this purpose was established not by ...ing the content of the tests and comparing it with the demands of ...mmar schools, but by establishing the correlation between the test scores and ...ccess in grammar school. If the students who did well on the tests did well at grammar school, in terms of success in public examinations, then the test was said to have *predictive validity*.

Predictive validity is often described as a type of *criterion-related validity*. There is a predictor – in the example above, the score on the 11 plus – and a criterion – success at grammar school. Establishing predictive validity requires showing that there is a good correlation between the predictor and the criterion. What 'good' means depends on the context. For example, it is common to find that tests of general intelligence taken at the age of 10 or 11 have a correlation of 0.7 with grades achieved on the GCSE five years later. In contrast, the correlation of A-level grades with degree class at British universities is much lower: around 0.3 to 0.4, but nothing else appears to predict degree class any better.

There is a second type of criterion-related validity, and that is *concurrent validity*. In the examples given above, the purpose of the predictor is to predict performance at some point in the future. However, there may be contexts when we are interested in the possibility of using one assessment to predict the performance on another assessment taken at the same time.

For example, to establish whether a student has a specific learning disability such as dyslexia, it is necessary for a trained psychologist to interview a student one-on-one for a substantial period of time, and conduct a range of psychological tests. The cost of such an assessment can run into hundreds of pounds for each student, and for this reason, many researchers have looked for assessment procedures that can be used in place of the individual interview. One such assessment is the Bangor Dyslexia System (Miles, 1998). This is a short test that can be administered quickly, and can be used to screen students for dyslexia. Students who do poorly on the screening test can then be given the more extensive interview to ascertain the precise nature of their disabilities.

Obviously, the important requirement of such a screening test is that it must be measuring the 'same thing' as the individual interview, otherwise it would be useless, and that is established through a concurrent validity study. A sample of students undergoes the extended one-on-one assessment with the trained psychologist, and they also take the screening test. If the results of the two assessments correlate reasonably well, then the short test can be used as a screening test for the psychologist interview. The criterion-related validation process will also yield evidence about where to make 'cut-scores' to make sure that students with dyslexia, but who score higher than expected on the screening test, do not get missed.

For many years these two forms of validity, content validity and criterion-related validity, dominated thinking about how to validate assessments. However, the validation of some forms of assessments, particularly in the area of personality psychology, didn't fit easily into either category. For example, if we had a questionnaire that was meant to measure someone's neuroticism, how could we check this? There is no clearly defined domain of questions that we could draw from, nor is it clear that neuroticism predicts anything. For that reason, interest focused on a third kind of validity – *construct validity*.

Early uses of construct validity centred on the idea of *convergent* and *discriminant* validity evidence. The idea here was that a measure of, say, neuroticism should correlate well with other measures of neuroticism (convergent evidence), but correlate less well with measures of, say, anxiety or agreeableness (discriminant evidence). In acknowledgement of the fact that they were inventions of psychologists, things like neuroticism and agreeableness were called 'constructs'. Validating the extent to which an assessment did measure the construct of interest was therefore called construct validity.

For a while, then, there was a 'holy trinity' of forms of validity – content, criterion-related and construct validity. Over time, however, researchers in assessment began to realize that the idea of construct validity really included the other two forms of validity, so that, in 1980, Samuel Messick, one of the leaders in the field, wrote that 'construct validity is indeed the unifying concept of validity that integrates criterion and content considerations into a common framework for testing rational hypotheses about theoretically relevant relationships' (Messick, 1980: 1015).

Around about the same time, it became clear that it was difficult to hold on to the idea of validity as a property of a test, since the test might be more valid for one group of students than for another. If we have a history test that has a high reading demand, then how do we make sense of the results? For students with good reading skills, then we might reasonably conclude that low scores on the test indicate that these students don't know much about history (or at least the aspects of history being tested). But for students with poor reading skills, we don't know whether low scores mean poor history knowledge, poor reading skills or both. We would be justified in drawing conclusions about history skills for some students (good readers) but not others (poor readers). The test would be a valid assessment for some students, but not others. Therefore *validity cannot be a property of a test*. Instead, validity is a property of inferences that we draw on the basis of assessment outcomes. Inferences about low history skills on the basis of low test scores might be warranted for the good readers (depending of course on the test) but not for the poor readers.

The idea bears some repeating, because the term 'validity' is so poorly understood and widely misused. There is no such thing as a valid test, not because perfection is unattainable (although this is true), but because validity is not a property of tests. Asking 'Is this a valid test?' makes no more sense than asking 'Is the moon selfish?' When someone asks, 'Is this a valid assessment?', the correct response is to say, 'Tell me what conclusions you propose to draw on the basis of the results of the assessment. Then we can look at whether there is evidence to justify such conclusions.'

Requirements for validity

As noted above, the purpose of any assessment is to allow us to look at the responses made by students and from those responses, make inferences beyond the specific aspects of the construct that were assessed. For these inferences to have any legitimacy, there are three specific requirements that have to be met. The assessment must have adequate reliability, it must address all important aspects of the construct about which we wish to generalize and the responses made by students must not be affected by factors irrelevant to the construct of interest. Each of these is discussed in turn below.

Reliability

No measurement is perfectly reliable. In the 20-item spelling test we discussed above, the actual score that Robin achieved would be affected by a number of factors. Given the same 20 words to spell later in the day, or earlier, Robin might do better, or worse. Given a different set of 20 words to spell from the list of 40, Robin might, again, do better, or worse. And depending on how neat his handwriting is, Robin's score might depend on who does the scoring, and the extent to which he is given the 'benefit of the doubt'.

A reliable test is one in which the scores that a student gets on different occasions, or with a slightly different set of questions on the test, or when someone else does the marking, does not change very much. By convention, a perfectly reliable test – impossible to achieve in practice – has a reliability of 1. It is impossible to achieve because to get a reliability of 1, it would have to be the case that every time a particular student was tested, she or he would get exactly the same score, no matter who did the marking, how the student felt or which particular questions were chosen in the test.

At the other extreme, a test with a reliability of 0 is completely unreliable. In other words, when the reliability is 0, the score that the student gets is just random. There is no information in the student score, or, what amounts to the same thing, we know no more about the student's ability after seeing the test result than we did before.

All real tests have reliabilities between these extremes. Tests and examinations used in schools, including public examinations like A-level and GCSE, typically have reliabilities between 0.75 and 0.85, while specialized psychological tests have reliabilities in the range 0.85 to 0.95. Interpreting these numbers, however, is far from straightforward. When a test has a reliability of 0.8, it does not mean that 80 per cent of the students get an accurate score on the test, nor even that the score is 80 per cent accurate. Rather, reliability is a kind of 'signal-to-noise' ratio for the test, which tells us how much information there is in the test about a specific student, and this is given in probabilistic terms.

In a class of 25 students, with a test whose reliability is 0.8, and with scores ranging from 20 per cent to 80 per cent, then on any given testing occasion two-thirds of students will get a score within 7 per cent of their long-run average (i.e. the average if they took the same, or a similar test, lots of times). This means that one-third of the students (i.e. eight students) will get a score that is more than 7 per cent from their long-term average, and one student in this class will get a score that is more than 14 per cent from their long-term average. The problem is that we don't know who these students are, and we don't know whether they got scores higher or lower than their long-term average. Given that most tests used in school have reliabilities around 0.8 (and most teacher-constructed tests have reliabilities well below this) it shows that we need to be very careful drawing any kinds of conclusions on the basis of a single test. For details of how these numbers were arrived at and for further practical examples of the impact of reliability on test scores, see Wiliam (2001).

Ensuring the construct is adequately represented

Even if the test is adequately reliable, there are other things that might threaten our ability to make inferences on the basis of test outcomes. One is the extent to which the test adequately represents the construct we are interested in. For example, when mathematics GCSE was introduced in 1988, the Examining Groups were required to include a coursework component in order to assess important aspects of mathematics that were not easily tested in timed, written examinations, such as investigative aspects of mathematics. The idea here was that if we wanted to be able to conclude, from someone's GCSE grade in mathematics, how good they are at mathematical investigations, then we had better include investigations in the assessment. In the same way, if the assessment of competence in English is about reading, writing and speaking and listening, then the assessment needs to represent all these aspects. If we only assess reading and writing, then any conclusions we draw about someone's ability to speak and listen are likely to be unwarranted, even though these are parts of the construct of English. In the technical language of assessment, an assessment of English that failed to assess speaking and listening would suffer from *construct under-representation*.

Eliminating irrelevant factors

If construct under-representation is when an assessment fails to include enough of the construct of interest, then the opposite problem is when the assessment includes things it shouldn't. So, in the example of the history test mentioned above, because the test had a high reading demand, we could not be sure whether students who did badly did so because they did not know the history being assessed, or because they could not read the question well enough. We want the differences between scores to be due to differences in the capability of the students with respect to the construct of history, and not to do with other factors that we deem irrelevant, such as reading ability. In our history test, some of the variation in the scores obtained by different students was due to differences in knowledge of history. But some of the variation was due to factors, such as reading, that are irrelevant to the construct we are interested in. In assessment, it is common to quantify the variation in scores in terms of a statistical measure called the variance. Therefore, our history assessment, or more precisely, inferences based on scores on our history assessment, would suffer from *construct-irrelevant variance*.

The relationship between the essential requirements

These three features of assessments – inadequate reliability, construct under-representation, and construct-irrelevant variance – are the main threats to being able to draw conclusions from test results, but the relationship between them is complex. For example, if we want to have reliable assessments, then one thing we could do is to use multiple choice tests. Because the scoring of multiple choice tests is not subject to differences in opinions between different markers, then they tend to be more reliable. And because multiple choice items tend to be short, then it is generally possible to ask lots of different questions, which again makes the test more reliable (because when you ask 50 questions, rather than five, it is unlikely that a student will be lucky in getting a set of items that particularly suit her or him). But the problem with multiple choice tests is that not all aspects of a construct can be tested. Increasing the reliability of a test can therefore result in increasing construct under-representation. Multiple choice questions may also weaken the validity of a test in another way. Because students are given potential answers in multiple choice items, many students can improve their scores through developing test-taking skills, such as eliminating clearly incorrect solutions, and then guessing between what's left. This kind of strategy can increase students' scores on a mathematics test, for example, without making them any better at mathematics. So some of the differences between their scores are due to differences in mathematical knowledge, and some of the differences are due to the test-taking ability. In other words, we have increased the construct-irrelevant variance. In our attempts to improve the validity of our inferences by reducing the unreliability, we have increased both the construct under-representation and the construct-irrelevant variance. Depending what conclusions we want to draw from the test results, 'improving' the test by increasing its reliability may actually make things worse.

One way to think about these three 'essential ingredients' of an assessment – ensuring adequate reliability while avoiding construct under-representation and construct-irrelevant variance – is by analogy with stage lighting. For a given power of illumination we can either focus this as a spotlight or as a floodlight. The spotlight brings real clarity to a small part of the stage, but the rest of the stage is in darkness. This is analogous to a highly reliable multiple choice test, in which the scores on the actual matter tested are highly reliable, but we know nothing about the other aspects of the domain that were not tested (construct under-representation). A floodlight, on the other hand, illuminates the whole stage. We may not be able to make quite such accurate distinctions in the small part of the domain assessed by the multiple choice test, but what we can say about the other areas will be *more* accurate. However, if our floodlight is cast too wide, we will illuminate parts of the theatre, such as the orchestra pit, that we did not want to illuminate (construct-irrelevant variance).

There is another advantage of defining validity as a property of inferences, rather than assessments, related to the issue of whether validity is objective or subjective. People often disagree about the validity of an assessment (more precisely, the inferences based on the assessment outcomes) because they disagree about the definition of the construct, rather than the validation process. For example some people define the construct of history to be about knowing facts and dates. For such proponents, multiple choice tests are a good way of testing history, and asking students to write essays in history exams weakens validity, because it introduces construct-irrelevant variance (in this case, differences in scores are partly attributable to history skill – which is relevant – but partly attributable to writing skill – which is deemed to be irrelevant). Others will disagree with this, seeing the central process of history as the assembling of historical argument, in which facts and dates are important, but not the whole story; the ability to reconcile conflicting sources, recognize bias in sources and other factors are also seen as relevant. From this second perspective, writing – generating historical argument – is central to the construct of history, and a multiple choice test will always under-represent this construct.

So the 'history as facts and dates' people advocate multiple choice tests, and the 'history as argument' people advocate essay-based tests. These two camps disagree about what history is all about, and they disagree about what assessments to use, but they do *not* disagree about the validity of each of the two forms of assessment. The 'history as facts and dates' camp agree that essay tests support inferences about the ability of students to assemble historical arguments better than do multiple choice tests; they just aren't interested in making these kinds of inferences because they don't think they have anything to do with history. Conversely, the 'history as argument' camp agree that multiple choice tests are better than essays in supporting inferences about students' mastery of facts and dates; they just think there's more to history than that. If validity were a property of tests, it would have to be subjective, depending on who did the judging. As a property of inferences, validity is objective, depending only on the quality of the evidence that connects the observations of assessment outcomes to the desired inferences.

The price we pay for this is that validation can never be completed. For example, we might have strong evidence that a particular test predicts performance at university well, but it might later emerge that the strength of the prediction is much less for some subgroups (e.g. students from minority ethnic communities) than for the generality of students. What seems like a safe inference at one point in time might turn out, in the light of new evidence, to be unwarranted. Further investigation might show that the reason that minority students do less well at university is that they experience more financial difficulties than other students, and when this is taken into account, the prediction for minority students is just as good as for the generality of students. Validation is thus a never-ending process of marshalling evidence that supports the inferences that we want to make from assessment outcomes, while at the same time, showing plausible rival inferences as less warranted. Thus validity is always provisional.

Interpreting assessments: norms, criteria and constructs

As should be clear by now, validity is all about the interpretations that we can legitimately draw from assessment results, but the question remains; what are these interpretations about? In the earliest days of assessments, the interpretations were just *cohort-referenced*. Recall Robin and Anita and the spelling test. As long as we just want to draw conclusions about the relative performance of students in the same class, then things are pretty straightforward. As long as our test has adequate reliability, and we are sure we are testing the spelling of words appropriate to the class, then we can say (within the limits of the reliability of the assessment) that Anita is better than Robin at spelling, or that Robin is average for the class. However, without more information, we cannot say whether Robin is average at spelling for students of that age. For that we need data on the performance of a representative sample of students of the same age on the same test. From these data we can construct tables of norms, which might indicate, for example, that

Robin's spelling ability is better than 40 per cent of students of the same age. This is a *norm-referenced* interpretation of a test score, and for most of the last century, most tests were designed to support norm-referenced interpretations. The problem with such norm-referenced interpretations is that the only requirement is that we can put students in rank order, and we can put students in rank order without having any idea what we are putting them in rank order *of*.

Dissatisfaction with this led, in the early 1960s, to the development of tests that could support criterion-referenced interpretations, and in particular, tests that would tell teachers what, specifically, students had and had not learned, so that teachers could take appropriate action. These tests were often called 'criterion-referenced tests', as if the distinction was inherent in the tests. However, since the same test could, if well designed, support both norm-referenced and criterion-referenced interpretations, then, like validity, the terms 'norm-referenced' and 'criterion-referenced' cannot be properties of tests. They are, like validity, properties of inferences based on assessment outcomes.

It is also important to note that tests designed to support criterion-referenced interpretations are themselves built on assumptions about norms. In the UK driving test, one criterion on which candidates have to show proficiency is 'Can cause the car to face in the opposite direction by means of the forward and reverse gears.' We know this as the 'three-point turn' even though in a narrow road, a five-point turn might well satisfy the examiner. However it seems highly unlikely that a 73-point turn would do so, even though it satisfies the letter of the criterion. All criteria are interpreted with respect to sets of norms, although these norms are often implicit.

Sometimes, the interpretation is made neither with respect to a set of norms, nor to a set of explicit criteria, but rather with respect to a construct shared by a group of individuals. Perhaps the best example of this is the grading of GCSE coursework in English, in which, through extensive 'agreement trialling' and debate, assessors have come to share a construct of quality in English (Marshall, 2000). Even though they may not be able to articulate why they agree, members of the community generally show close agreement about the value of a piece of work or a portfolio. Such interpretations of student work are *construct-referenced*.

Bias in assessment

There is no such thing as a biased test. This is because, like validity, bias is not a property of tests, but rather of conclusions we draw on the basis of test results. A test tests what a test tests. No more and no less. The bias creeps in when we try to draw inferences on the basis of test outcomes that are more warranted for some students than others. To understand this, it is instructive to consider what happens when an item is found to be much more difficult for one subgroup of students than another.

A mathematics teacher gives a 20-item test to her class. She scores the test, and finds that one particular item is answered correctly by ten of the 15 boys and five of the 15 girls in the class. One explanation of this could be that the boys in the class are just better than the girls at mathematics. In order to investigate this, the teacher calculates the total score for each student and finds that on average, the girls' and the boys' scores are equal. So, this item appears to be easier for boys than for girls of the same average achievement level in mathematics. It turns out that the item was testing the ability to rotate mentally a 3-D shape, and it is well known that, in most cultures, males are significantly better than females at this kind of item (Willingham and Cole, 1997). In the light of such 'differential item functioning', some people conclude that the item is biased against girls, but the item is *not* biased against girls because, as stated earlier, bias is not a property of tests or items. The item cannot be biased because it is simply testing the ability to rotate mentally a 3-D solid. It just tests what it tests. We may not like it, but if it turns out that boys are better than girls at this skill, then this is a fact about the world. Wishing it were otherwise will not change it.

Where the bias *does* come in is in the conclusions that people draw from such items, or tests that contain such items. To conclude that girls are less suited to study of advanced mathematics because they are less good at mental rotation *is* a biased inference. It is an inference for which there is no evidence. And for that reason, we might drop the item from the test. Not because the item is biased – it isn't – but because people might draw unwarranted conclusions on the basis of the test outcomes. The risk we run in dropping the item, however, is that we might end up with tests that substantially under-represent the construct of mathematics. For example, if we found out that girls find physics items harder than boys do, and boys find biology items harder than girls do, do we drop all these items from science tests and just test chemistry? There is no simple answer to issues such as these. However, a clear focus on validity and bias as properties of inferences, rather than of tests, helps us think things through more clearly.

Meanings and consequences of assessments

The argument so far – that validity is a never-ending process of marshalling evidence that our desired inferences are more justified than plausible rival inferences – represents an essentially static conception of the process of validation. While the process of validation is never completed, and there is always more to discover, there is nevertheless an assumption that the relationship between the inferences and the evidence should not be changing. This assumption is unlikely to be warranted when tests are used in social settings to make high-stakes determinations about students or teachers.

For example, there is widespread agreement that experimental skills such as observation, measurement and understanding safety in the laboratory are important parts of school science. When we look at someone's score on a science assessment, we want to be able to make inferences about all aspects of science, including experimental skills. The problem is that assessing these skills validly is difficult. Doing even one experiment takes a lot of time, and the reliability of student scores are affected by a number of things. First, a student may have a good day, or a bad day (e.g. from hay fever). Second, with only one teacher in the room to observe the students' practical skills, any scores awarded will depend on the skill of the teacher, and her or his understanding of the scoring guide. Third, with only one task, that particular task may suit some students well, so they get a higher score than they would get on other experiments, while other students may get a lower score than they would on other experiments. Indeed, some people have argued that because of these difficulties, we should not bother with practical assessments at all. They point out that the correlation between the scores on practical tasks and on paper and pencil tests is very high. Their argument is therefore that if we know the scores obtained on a suitable paper and pencil test we are safe in making inferences about practical skills (this is, of course, an argument about the concurrent validity of the paper and pencil tests and practical tasks).

However, there is a high correlation between practical skills and pencil and paper tests only because teachers have ensured a balance of practical and theoretical elements in their teaching. As pressure to increase test results grows, more emphasis is placed on the aspects of performance that are assessed in the tests. Teachers then spend less time on practical work, so the correlation between practical skills and scores on pencil and paper tests declines. Scores on pencil and paper tests are then no longer a good proxy for experimental skills, and inferences about practical skills made on the basis of just pencil and paper test scores are likely to be just wrong. For this reason, recent work on validity has taken much more account of the social consequences of assessments, and the impact that these have on the meaning of assessment scores. In order to validate an assessment, we need therefore to consider both the meanings of assessment outcomes, and their consequences.

Conclusion

This chapter has emphasized that validity is the key concept in evaluating the quality of assessments, and has stressed the need to think about validity not as a property of tests, but as a property of the inferences that we make on the basis of test scores. Early work in this area focused on particular kinds of validity such as content validity, criterion-related validity (which included predictive and concurrent validity) and construct validity, but over time, validity came to be seen much more holistically as 'an overall evaluative judgement of the adequacy and appropriateness of inferences and actions based on test scores' (Messick, 1988: 42). The major threats to making sound inferences are that the scores are not stable enough (unreliability), the assessments fail to assess things we want to make inferences about (construct under-representation) or mix up things we care about with things we don't (construct-irrelevant variance). We can make inferences with respect to norms, criteria or shared understandings (constructs), and although these inferences can be biased, the tests themselves cannot. More importantly, the kinds of inferences that we can make, and their stability, will be affected, sometimes radically, by the social settings in which tests are used.

Points for reflection

The idea of evaluating assessments in terms of the inferences they support, rather than the assessments themselves, takes some getting used to, but it's well worth it in terms of the clarity it brings to one's thinking. Below are some statements about assessment. If I have succeeded in my aim in writing this chapter, you will be able to see what is wrong with each of them. If I have been really successful, you will be able to rephrase each of the statements in terms of the concepts developed in this chapter.

- 'IQ tests are biased against working class students.'
- 'English GCSE is not valid.'
- 'Including mental rotation problems biases mathematics tests against girls.'
- 'There aren't enough physics questions in this test for it to be a valid science test.'
- 'The fact that national curriculum test scores in English at key stage 2 have gone up while reading test scores have gone down shows that the national curriculum tests are not valid.'

Notes

1. This title is taken from a chapter by Angoff (1988).
2. In this chapter the term 'test' is used as a generic term for any kind of formal assessment procedure, including examinations and assessment tasks.

Further reading

Messick, S. (1989) 'Validity', in R.L. Linn (ed.) *Educational Measurement* (3rd edn), Washington, DC: American Council on Education/Macmillan.

Wainer, H. and Braun, H.I. (eds) (1988) *Test Validity*, Hillsdale, NJ: Lawrence Erlbaum Associates.

Wiliam, D. (1992) 'Some technical issues in assessment: a user's guide', *British Journal for Curriculum and Assessment*, 2: 11–20.

—— (2001) 'Reliability, validity and all that jazz', *Education 3–13*, 29: 17–21.

References

Angoff, W.H. (1988) 'Validity: an evolving concept', in H. Wainer and H.I. Braun (eds) *Test Validity*, Hillsdale, NJ: Lawrence Erlbaum Associates.

Cronbach, L.J. (1971) 'Test validation', in R.L. Thorndike (ed.) *Educational Measurement* (2nd edn), Washington DC: American Council on Education.

Kelley, T.L. (1927) *The Interpretation of Educational Measurement*, Yonkers, NY: World Book Company.

Marshall, B. (2000) *English Teachers – the Unofficial Guide: researching the philosophies of English teachers*, London: RoutledgeFalmer.

Messick, S. (1980) 'Test validity and the ethics of assessment', *American Psychologist*, 35: 1012–27.

—— (1988) 'The once and future issues of validity: assessing the meaning and consequences of measurement', in H. Wainer and H.I. Braun (eds), *Test Validity*, Hillsdale, NJ: Lawrence Erlbaum Associates.

Miles, E. (1998) *The Bangor Dyslexia Teaching System*, London: Whurr.

Wiliam, D. (2001) 'Reliability, validity and all that jazz', *Education 3–13*, 29: 17–21.

Willingham, W.S. and Cole, N.S. (eds) (1997) *Gender and Fair Assessment*, Mahwah, NJ: Lawrence Erlbaum Associates.

Trusting teachers' judgement

Wynne Harlen

> How can evidence that is gathered and used to help learning also be used to build a picture summarizing learning at a particular time?

Some of the questions often asked about classroom assessment are: How do formative assessment and summative assessment relate to each other? Is there a real difference between them – or is there just 'good assessment'? In attempting to answer these questions it is important to keep in mind that formative assessment (or assessment for learning) and summative assessment (or assessment of learning) refer to different purposes of assessment, not to types of evidence or methods of gathering evidence. We are, therefore, essentially concerned with how best to serve these purposes.

This chapter is about the relationship between formative and summative assessment, and, in particular, how evidence that is gathered and used to help learning can also be used to build a picture summarizing learning at a particular time. Since such a dual use of evidence depends upon the teacher having responsibility for summative assessment as well as for formative assessment it follows that we must be able to trust teachers' judgements of pupils' achievement. The implications of this are quite profound. For this reason, following a brief review of similarities and differences between formative and summative assessment the chapter sets out a case for using teachers' judgements for summative assessment. This is followed by a discussion on how evidence gathered as part of teaching and used formatively can be reviewed and judged against criteria for reporting achievement and how the reliability of these judgements can be optimized. In conclusion we return to the nature of the distinction between formative and summative assessment.

Purposes and uses of assessment

Assessment for different purposes

As other chapters in this book make clear, formative assessment is essentially carried out by teachers as part of teaching. It should be an ongoing and regular part of the teacher's role. However, the fact of being carried out regularly does not mean that the assessment serves to help learning. Regular tests are not necessarily formative in function; it depends on how the results are used and who uses them. So what is needed to serve the different purpose of formative and summative assessment?

For formative assessment key aspects are that:

- evidence is gathered about ongoing learning activities that can be used to make decisions about how to help further learning.
- the evidence is judged in terms of progress towards the detailed lesson goals; these goals may vary for different individual pupils or for groups and so comparisons between pupils are not sensible or justified.
- pupils are aware of their lesson goals and can help in deciding their next steps towards the goals.
- the process is cyclical and ongoing, information being gathered and used as an integral part of teaching and learning.
- no judgement of grade or level is involved; only the judgement of how to help a student take the next steps in learning, so reliability is not an issue. Information is gathered frequently by teachers who will be able to use feedback to correct any mistaken judgement.

Making a judgement about how far pupils have reached in terms of overall goals or levels is not a purpose of formative assessment, but it is the purpose of summative assessment. Another key distinction between assessment that serves these two purposes is that in formative assessment the concern is to help progress at a detailed level, whereas in summative assessment the concern is to judge achievement against broader indicators, such as level descriptions or grade level criteria. This is the difference between, for example, helping pupils to recognize the features of earthworms that show adaptation to their particular habitat and assessing how well they understand how animals and plants are suited to their environments. We return later to this relationship between goals at different levels of generality in the context of using teachers' judgements for summative purposes.

Since the purpose of summative assessment is to summarize and report achievement at a particular time, its main characteristics are:

- the process takes place at a particular time, it is not ongoing and not cyclical
- the evidence used relates to the same goals for all pupils

- the evidence is interpreted in terms of publicly available criteria
- the judgement is reported in terms of levels, grades or scores, which need to be underpinned by some quality assurance procedures
- pupils have a limited role, if any, in the process.

Different uses of assessment outcomes

A further difference between formative assessment and summative assessment lies in the ways in which the outcomes are used. In formative assessment, there is one use of the outcome, to help learning; if not used in this way, the assessment is not formative. On the other hand, outcomes of summative information about pupil achievement are used in various different ways: for internal school tracking of pupils' progress; informing parents, pupils and the pupils' next teachers of what has been achieved; certification or accreditation of learning by an external body; or selection. These can be grouped into two main uses – 'internal' and 'external' to the school community:

- 'internal' uses include using regular grading, record keeping, informing decisions about courses to follow where there are options within the school, reporting to parents and to the students themselves
- 'external' uses include certification by examination bodies or for vocational qualifications, selection for further or higher education.

In addition, the aggregated results from the assessment of individual pupils are frequently used in other ways, which have less direct, but nonetheless serious consequences for their education. The more important of these is the use of summative assessment results for the evaluation of teachers, schools and local authorities. This use raises the 'stakes' of the assessment for the teachers and leads to summative assessment influencing the curriculum and teaching methods. There is a considerable body of research evidence of teachers teaching to the test and using transmission methods of teaching in response to being set targets in terms of numbers of pupils achieving specific levels or scores (Crooks, 1988; Black and Wiliam, 1998; Johnston and McClune, 2000; ARG, 2004). The impact of this on pupils can be to reduce their motivation for learning, produce anxiety that prevents some from performing as well as they can and promoting shallow learning that enables them to pass tests rather than the 'deeper' learning needed for understanding and cognitive skill development (Harlen and Deakin Crick, 2003).

The potential for serving more than one purpose

The above lists of characteristics of formative and summative assessment suggest a sharp distinction between these purposes. Does this necessarily mean that the evidence collected for one purpose cannot be used for the other? Two particular questions arise: Can evidence collected to summarize learning be used to help learning? Can evidence collected and used to help learning be used for summative purposes?

In relation to the first of these questions, the starting point is summary information about the achievement of overall goals. In this case, the extent to which this information can be related to detailed learning goals is limited, particularly when the outcomes are in the form of test scores. Some uses of test results are described by Black *et al.* (2003) as formative. These include using past test items to focus revision, involving pupils in setting tests and teachers using results to identify areas needing further attention. However, the opportunities for such uses cannot be so frequent as to be described as 'ongoing' or a regular part of teaching and learning, as required for formative assessment. Further, although there is opportunity to feed back summative information into teaching when it is conducted internally to the school, in general the information does not have the detail that is needed to help specific learning. Although theoretically possible to obtain and use information from marked scripts from external tests and examinations, teachers generally only use their own tests for feedback into teaching.

The second question relates to using information from formative assessment for summative assessment. This process does not suffer from the same disadvantages just noted for the reverse process, although it is not necessarily without problems. Formative assessment makes use of a mass of detailed evidence, which can be collapsed to provide the more general description of achievement, as required for summative purposes. The difficulties arise because formative assessment provides evidence that is unwieldy and often inconsistent, since what pupils can do is affected by the context, which changes from one activity to another. These differences, useful in helping learning (because they indicate the conditions that seem to help or inhibit learning), are regarded as sources of error in summarizing learning. When these problems are overcome, as we see later, the use of evidence from formative assessment allows the full range of pupils' experiences to be represented in the account of their achievements. This contrasts with the account provided by tests that necessarily can only sample the range of knowledge, understanding, skills and non-cognitive goals of education.

The case for using teachers' judgements for summative assessment

In addition to those points already noted, there are several other problems associated with using tests and examinations, whether external or teacher-made, for summative assessment. Some of these are severe enough to make it imperative to look for alternatives. In the present context, a particularly serious result of frequent use of tests and examinations assessment is their impact on the practice of formative assessment. As pointed out in an Assessment Reform Group booklet:

> Assessing pupils frequently in terms of levels or grades means that the feedback that they get is predominantly judgemental encouraging them to compare themselves with others. In such circumstances there is little attention by teachers or pupils to the formative use of assessment.
>
> (ARG, 2006a: 10)

Here we ask: would summative assessment conducted in some other way, such as by using teachers' judgements, fare any better? To address this question it is important to be clear about the basis for making a comparison.

What properties should any summative assessment have? First, it is essential for an assessment that summarizes learning to provide an account of achievement that is valid and reliable.

- Being valid means that what is assessed corresponds with the behaviours or learning outcomes that it is intended should be assessed. This is crucial because what is assessed exerts a strong influence on what learning is valued.
- Being reliable refers to how consistent the results are, regardless of who conducts the assessment or the particular occasion or circumstances at the time.

The degree to which an assessment needs to be reliable depends on the use of the result. The need for high reliability is less in the case of internal uses of summative assessment, which do not involve comparisons between or selection of pupils, than for external uses or when pupils are being selected for courses.

Validity and reliability of the outcome are not the only desirable properties of summative assessment. It is also important to consider the impact of the process on other parts of the system and on pupils and teachers. For example, how summative assessment for external uses is conducted influences teachers' own internal summative assessment. The impact is made more serious by teachers who, in their anxiety to achieve target numbers of pupils reaching certain levels or grades, give pupils frequent tests of their own or use commercial tests. (The number of tests purchased in the UK soared after the introduction of national testing in the early 1990s.) Thus what could be a relatively infrequent experience of tests, at key points across the years, became a regular part of pupils' experience, and one not enjoyed by most.

A further, somewhat related, matter is the cost of the process, both in terms of time for teaching and learning and direct costs. After all it would be possible in theory to increase the reliability of tests and examinations by double or triple marking all the answers, but the costs would be prohibitive.

So the pros and cons of different approaches to summative assessment need to be evaluated in terms of validity, reliability, impact and cost. We now consider the extent to which tests and teachers' judgements meet the required properties.

Validity: is what is assessed what ought to be assessed?

As noted earlier, most tests and examinations can address only some learning goals, and those partially, and may entirely neglect others such as higher thinking skills, personal qualities and non-academic achievement. However, most who receive the results, the 'users' of assessment, want to see evidence of both academic and non-academic achievement. Both employers and higher education admission tutors want to be able to identify those who are independent learners, who show initiative and perseverance and have learned how to learn. Reporting such outcomes when pupils leave school is not enough; the progress towards them needs to be monitored throughout school. Consequently such outcomes ought to be included in summative assessment, if it is to give a valid account of learning, as well as in formative assessment.

The more important the decisions that rest on the assessment result, the greater the degree of reliability that is required, and this has consequences for validity. Validity is threatened when concern for reliability leads to a reduction in how well what is assessed reflects the range of achievement that is intended and required by users of the assessment outcome. This happens when, in the development of the test or examination, there is a preference for items relating to outcomes that are most reliably assessed. Often this results from the 'high stakes' given to test results when they are used as accountability measures. There is then pressure for tests to be as 'objective' as possible since there is a premium on reliable marking in the interests of fairness. Then a test, which is only a small sample of learning outcomes in any case, is not in fact a good sample of the range but only of those parts that are readily and reliably assessed in this way. These most often include factual knowledge, where answers can be marked unequivocally, and exclude what is more difficult to judge, such as application of knowledge, critical reasoning and affective outcomes. Examples are some science practical examinations that take the form of routine procedures and make little cognitive demand on pupils, but are easily scored.

Use of evidence gathered and judged by teachers can improve the match between the range of intended learning and the information provided by the assessment since, as part of their regular work, teachers can build up a picture of pupils' attainment across the full ranges of activities and goals. This gives a broader and fuller account of achievement than can be obtained through tests. Also, freedom from test anxiety means that the assessment is a more valid indication of achievement.

In some circumstances it may be desirable for teachers' judgements to be supplemented by information from externally devised tasks or tests. The reason may be that these tasks present the best way of providing evidence of certain skills or understanding, or that the use of the assessment data requires a greater degree of uniformity in how the assessment is conducted than is found in teachers' assessment data. A well designed set of assessment tasks available for teachers to use has several benefits. Such tasks can exemplify for teachers the situations in which skills and understanding are used and thus guide them in developing their own embedded assessment tasks. They are also of particular benefit to newly qualified teachers and those who need to build their confidence in their ability to assess students.

Reliability: how closely could the result be reproduced?

External tests and examinations are generally assumed to be reliable, but this assumption is not borne out by the facts. Black and Wiliam point out the consequences in firm words:

> … the public in general and policy-makers in particular do not pay attention to reliability. They appear to have faith in the dependability of the results of short tests when they are in fact ignorant of the sizes of inescapable errors that accompany this and any other measure.
>
> (Black and Wiliam, 2006: 119)

Black and Wiliam go on to estimate the proportion of pupils who are likely to be misclassified by tests at KS2 and KS3, in England, assuming a test reliability of 0.8, as 32 per cent and 43 per cent respectively. They also point out that to increase the reliability of the tests and reduce the percentages misclassified would require an increase in the length of the test far beyond what is acceptable, adding that 'Fortunately, there is another way of increasing the effective length of a test, without increasing testing time, and that is through the use of teacher assessment' (Black and Wiliam, 2006: 126).

Assessment by teachers has the potential for providing information about a wide range of cognitive and affective outcomes but the reliability of teachers' judgements is widely held to be low and there is research evidence of bias. However, the research (Harlen, 2005) also shows that when criteria are well specified (and understood) teachers are able to make judgements of acceptable reliability. The moderation procedures that are required for quality assurance can be conducted in a way that provides quality enhancement of teaching and learning, as discussed later.

Impact: what are the consequences for teaching and learning?

What is assessed, and how, will always have an impact on teaching. The impact can be positive if the assessment covers the full range of intended goals, when the assessment criteria often help to clarify the meaning of the goals. However the impact on learning experiences can be restrictive if there is a mismatch between the intended curriculum and the scope of the assessment. The consequences are likely to be more severe when results are used for accountability of teachers and schools. It is these uses that raise the 'stakes' of pupil assessment and lead to summative assessment having a narrowing influence on the curriculum and teaching methods, as noted earlier.

Basing summative assessment on teachers' judgements gives teachers greater freedom to pursue learning goals in ways that suit their pupils rather than using the methods that are assumed to lead to good test performance and the same methods for all. This is related to their greater freedom to use assessment to help learning, for when teachers do this they recognize the different help that pupils need and they can be creative in providing it. Unfortunately using tests for summative assessment leads to teachers using tests for their own assessments; they are not encouraged nor given the skills to use their own judgements.

The impact of the way that external summative assessment is conducted on how teachers conduct their own assessment has already been mentioned. The research by Pollard *et al.* (2000) showed that, following the introduction of external tests in the primary school, teachers' own classroom assessment became more summative. Pupils were aware of a change of their teachers' assessment, which focused more on performance than on learning processes, and they reported that it gave them less help than before. As a further consequence, pupils themselves began to adopt summative criteria in assessing their own work. Using teachers' judgements will not necessarily ensure more formative use of assessment by teachers but it makes it possible. Many teachers recognize the values of formative assessment but feel unable to make the change in their teaching style that it requires, when struggling to improve test scores.

An increased role for pupils in their own assessment is made possible by using teachers' judgements for summative assessment. Formative assessment requires that pupils are aware of their learning goals for a lesson or section of work. This can be extended, certainly for older pupils, to knowledge of longer-term goals and realizing what they are aiming for in terms of learning, rather than performance on tests. Openness about goals and criteria for assessment not only helps pupils to direct their effort appropriately but removes the secrecy from the process of summative assessment, enabling them to recognize their own role in their achievement instead of it being the result of someone else's decisions.

Cost: what time and other resources are required?

Estimating costs in education is notoriously difficult; trying to disentangle time spent on assessment from other activities is even more difficult. However some very rough estimates attempted by the Assessment Systems for the Future project (ARG, 2006b) for the years 2003–5, suggest that, in the primary school in England, teachers' time spent on all assessment-related tasks, including teachers' assessment, moderation, report writing, parents' evenings and national testing where appropriate, varied from 130 hours per year in Year 1 to 160 hours in Year 6. Teachers' time spent specifically on testing (both internal and external) varied from 0 hours in Year 1 to 20 hours per year in Year 6. The actual time spent on national testing was much smaller than the time spent on regular tests given by the teacher, the difference being the result of teachers giving students practice tests and generally using tests in preference to their own judgements. Of course fewer tests and more assessment by teachers would increase the need for moderation. However, the time saved in testing would more than compensate for the time necessary to provide half a day every three weeks for moderation activities. Pupils' time could be increased by at least two weeks a year by using class work rather than tests to assess progress.

In terms of direct costs, although the direct cost to schools of national tests is small, there would be considerable savings at the school level by purchasing fewer commercial tests for practice. At the secondary level, however, the cost of external examination fees is considerable, estimated at over £100,000 per year for an 11–18 school (revised to an £400,000 in 2006) (ARG, 2006b). An estimate for the cost of tests and assessment to the system in England, for 2003 was £610 million (PWC, 2004).

Using evidence for formative and summative assessment

Here we consider how in practice evidence gathered and used in helping learning can also be used as a basis for reporting on learning. We begin with an example and then offer a view in terms of a general framework, or model, of how the process can be used in other situations. We also consider ways in which the necessary safeguards of reliability can be built into the assessment procedures.

An example from practice

This example draws upon work described in a package of material produced in Scotland to support teachers in using diagnostic assessment to help pupils learn science (SCRE, 1995). Similar packages were produced for mathematics and language. The activity described is one commonly undertaken in science, where questions relating to camouflage in animals are being investigated. The 10–11-year-old pupils worked in groups to plan and carry out investigations, which involved placing cut-out animal shapes painted in different colours against different backgrounds. The teacher's goals for the activity related both to the understanding to be developed and to the development of skills of investigation.

In relation to the conceptual development, the ideas about camouflage were the 'small' ideas that could be expected to be extended through this particular activity. The development of longer-term 'big' ideas, of why different living things are found in different environments, would depend on linking together several small ideas from different activities. These might involve thinking about the requirements of living things for food and water, for instance.

As the activities progressed the teacher discussed their ideas with the pupils as she visited the groups, probing their understanding of why some colours and shapes were easier than others to see against different backgrounds. She also challenged them to apply their emerging ideas to different situations by questions such as about the likely differences between the habitats of white bears and brown bears.

In relation to the development of skills of investigation, the activities gave opportunities for a range of enquiry skills to be used. The teacher observed their actions and listened to their talk as they planned and carried out their investigations, occasionally asking for explanations of their reasons for how they were doing certain things. In this way she gathered evidence that could be used to help in developing their enquiry skills. For example, in relation to their planning, Ben appeared to be ready for addressing his own question, whilst Anna need more help in relating actions to the question selected.

> Ben, (who had shown a clear idea of how to carry out the investigation in the way selected) would be helped by being asked to think of different ways of approaching the investigation. What do you want to find out from your investigations? Can you put this in the form of a question you want to answer? In what ways could you set about answering this question?
>
> Anna (who had not shown a good grasp of what was being tested in the investigation) would benefit from being challenged to give reasons for her planned actions and to distinguish between things which are important to the investigation and those which are not. Was it important that this was done in this way? Why? If someone else were going to do this what would be the most important things to tell them?
>
> (SCRE, 1995: 23)

Thus during the activities, evidence was used formatively to help learning. Then, at the end of the year, when it was necessary to report progress in terms of levels achieved, the teacher reviewed the evidence from the camouflage and other science activities. For both the conceptual goals and the enquiry skills goals, evidence from different specific activities had to be brought together so as to form an overall judgement for each pupil about where he or she had reached in development of the 'bigger' ideas and more generalized skills. The teacher did this by reviewing the evidence against the criteria for reporting levels of attainment. Did the work of Ben and Anna match the relevant criteria for levels C, D or E (the grading used in Scotland where the work was carried out)? The criteria used were related to skills in science and understanding of the interaction of living things with their environment within the overall outcome relating to living things and process of life. Criteria in other main conceptual areas were used for physical science topics covered during the year. In some cases the most recent evidence would predominate, but not invariably, since content areas visited earlier in the year may not have been revisited and in any case the use of enquiry skill is influenced by the subject matter of the enquiry.

The evidence reviewed in forming the judgement would be from the pupil's notebooks and other products, the teacher's jotted notes of observations and her notes that recorded how evidence was used to adapt teaching in response to ongoing formative assessment.

Modelling the process

Figure 9.1 attempts to describe in general terms the process illustrated in the example just discussed.

In the centre column are the activities conducted over the period of time for which achievement is being reported. On the left-hand side are the detailed lesson goals and the criteria used in formative assessment by teacher and pupils to judge next steps and how to take them. On the right-hand side are the broad cri-

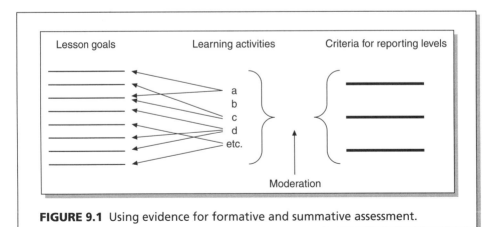

FIGURE 9.1 Using evidence for formative and summative assessment.

teria that define reporting levels for the major attainment outcomes. In the example, one set of reporting criteria would relate to skills of investigation and others to ideas about living things and perhaps to physical science if relevant activities have been undertaken during the year.

Placing the learning activities in the centre of the model indicates that the evidence they provide about pupils' learning is used in two ways, for formative assessment and for summative assessment. It must be emphasized that what is used in both cases is evidence, not judgements, about whether individual learning goals were or were not achieved; the same evidence is used prospectively to help current and future learning and retrospectively to report on past learning. The summative assessment is not a summation or average of a series of judgements. It is important that it is a holistic process, not an atomistic one such as using a tick list. Only in this way can it be ensured that all important learning outcomes, not just an easily assessed subset, are included.

Comparison with current practice

How is this different from the way in which teachers conduct their 'teacher assessment' as required for national assessment? Current practice is often driven by pressures of being held responsible for ensuring that pupils make regular and visible progress. The response to these pressures is to resort to frequent summative assessment, often in the form of teacher-made or commercial tests in order to supply evidence of progress. The pressures can be, however, less real than supposed and certainly much greater than they need be if schools and education authorities made efforts to communicate to parents and others how assessment is being used to help learning at all times and that this is hindered by frequent summative assessment. It also needs to be appreciated that children's learning is not regular and that change in important skills and understanding takes time; it is no accident that levels of achievement in most curricula are about two years apart. To attempt to detect change at more frequent intervals results in focusing on 'surface' learning, such as memorizing facts that are quickly learned and just as quickly forgotten, and in frequent tests to demonstrate this 'learning'.

The practice of dividing the intervals between levels within the curriculum into a number of sub-levels, so that pupils supposedly advance by three of these sub-levels per year, flies in the face of what is known about how pupils learn. It creates a spurious need for regular summative assessment so that checks can be made on whether the required progress is being made. These checks are primarily summative assessments, aimed at deciding the sub-levels or 'points' achieved by pupils in between levels. Sadly, because these assessments occur so often, they are assumed to be formative, but in reality they are a succession of summative assessments. They are insufficiently detailed and too narrow to help learning, and mean that opportunity is missed for using assessment formatively and so raising standards.

To avoid these effects requires two important policy changes. One is to cease to 'rely solely, or even mainly, on the data derived from summative assessment of pupils. Such data should be reported, and interpreted, in the context of the broad set of indicators of school effectiveness' (ARG, 2006a: 12). This would reduce the 'stakes' and allow summative assessment to have the role intended, that is, to report for individual pupils on all the skills, knowledge and understanding that are the aims of the curriculum. The other is to require summative assessment only when reports are needed, at the end of a year or half-year, or when major decisions have to be made. At other times assessment should be formative.

Enhancing the reliability of teachers' judgements

The process of forming an overall judgement from evidence collected over time is not a particularly tidy one. The evidence from different activities, as mentioned earlier, is often inconsistent and fragmentary. This is not a problem for formative assessment, but for summative purposes the unevenness has to be smoothed out. This is where the 'best fit' approach comes in. It involves accepting that 'not every piece of work will meet the criteria and not every criterion at the "best fit" level will be met' (Harlen and James, 1997: 374). But it also draws attention to the need for some quality assurance procedure to be included so that the results are seen to be dependable. This generally means some form of moderation of judgements, indicated in Figure 9.1 by the arrow between the evidence and the summative judgement of level. The greater the importance attached to the result, the higher the 'stakes', the more stringent the moderation procedures need to be. For 'internal' uses of summative assessment within-school moderation procedures may be sufficient. But for 'external' uses, procedures are needed that ensure that judgements made in different schools are fair and comparable.

The most valuable form of moderation takes place when teachers meet to discuss together their judgements of evidence relating to individual students. Given the point just made about the unevenness of the evidence this should be in the form of a portfolio of evidence of all kinds, including the student's work and the teacher's notes. In discussing specific examples, teachers share and align their interpretation of criteria and refine their future judgements as well as arriving at agreed results for the examples considered. There are two further advantages of this process. First, the benefits go beyond the assessment and extend to a better understanding of learning goals and how to work towards them. Second, it makes clear to all involved that assessment is not a process that leads to an exact result. This is universally true for all assessment, but is concealed by the apparent precision of scores on a test, even though these do not have any exact meaning in terms of what has been learned or even what can and cannot be done.

When teachers cannot easily meet to discuss examples, a second-best moderation approach is to provide a bank of examples, in the form of portfolios already assessed and with notes on what are the significant aspects that lead to the judgement that it is evidence of one level of attainment rather than another. The danger in this approach is that the examples become guidelines for activities so that the assessment criteria can be easily applied. Another form of moderation uses a bank of externally devised tasks or tests, developed and verified as indicating specific levels, that teachers can use to check their own judgements. There is clearly the danger in the use of such a bank that the tasks or tests come to be seen as most important and influence teaching. It is important that they are seen as part of the evidence that teachers use in forming their judgements.

Perhaps the best way of ensuring care and accuracy in the process and confidence in the outcome of teachers' judgements is to make the assessment procedures as transparent as possible. Sharing criteria and making clear the variety and range of evidence that is used means that the fairness of the outcomes can be judged by users of assessment information, such as parents, pupils, other teachers, employers and those in further and higher education. A wider understanding of assessment should include how it helps learning, as well as reporting on it. This brings us back to the theme of this chapter, the relationship between the formative and summative purposes of assessment.

Conclusion

The example and the discussion of using teachers' judgements for summative assessment have underlined the point that the same evidence can be used for formative and for summative assessment. What distinguishes between them is how that evidence is interpreted to serve the different purposes. Evidence, such as how a child goes about planning a science investigation, or what words he or she can or cannot read, is only useful when it is interpreted against some expectation or standard, embodied in the assessment criteria. It then becomes information about where the child is in relation to the goals of learning. The representation in Figure 9.1 shows that the criteria used in formative and summative assessment are different – formative to the left and summative to the right in the figure.

The criteria used in formative assessment will be partially child-referenced, that is, specific to the development of the individual pupil. This means that the same evidence may be interpreted differently for different pupils. If this were not the case, then lower achieving pupils would be constantly faced with failure. Instead, the information can be used to help progress of each one without reference to where other pupils have reached.

For summative assessment, however, the same criteria are used for all pupils, so that users of the information know what has been achieved. This involves recognizing that some pupils are further ahead than others. This is one of the reasons for arguing that summative assessment should not be conducted frequently but only when reports are necessary. It also needs to be handled sensitively so that 'when they don't have skills or knowledge, or they're behind other students, this is not a sign of deep, shameful deficit. It's a sign that they need to study harder or find new learning strategies' (Dweck, 1999: 129).

So, as long as we find it useful to define different purposes for assessment, it is important to recognize the different processes that are needed to serve these purposes. When these processes involve using teachers' judgements, valid information can be obtained with minimal negative impact on pupils and on schools' resources. As in the case of all assessment, information based on teachers' judgements is subject to error. But, as we have noted, moderation procedures that lead to more dependable summative assessment can be conducted so that they have a professional development function as well as improving the interpretation and use of evidence. A better understanding of the processes of assessment can only be of benefit also to formative assessment.

Points for reflection

1. What changes in procedures for assessment of learning would protect the use of assessment for learning?
2. What are the greatest obstacles to making more and better use of teachers' judgements for assessing learning?
3. How can these obstacles be overcome?

Further reading

ASF/ARG (2006) *The Role of Teachers in the Assessment of Learning*, Assessment Reform Group. Available from the CPA Office, Institute of Education, University of London. Online, available at: www.assessment-reform-group.org (accessed 10 July 2007).

Harlen, W. (2005) 'Teachers' summative practices and assessment for learning: tensions and synergies', *Curriculum Journal*, 16: 207–22.

—— (2006) 'On the relationship between assessment for formative and summative purposes', in J. Gardner (ed.) *Assessment and Learning*, London: Sage.

References

ARG (2004) *Testing, Motivation and Learning*. Available from the CPA Office, Institute of Education, University of London. Online, available at: www.assessment-reform-group.org (accessed 10 July 2007).

—— (2006a) *The Role of Teachers in the Assessment of Learning*, available from the CPA Office, Institute of Education, University of London. Online, available at: www.assessment-reform-group.org (accessed 10 July 2007).

—— (2006b) *Assessment Systems for the Future Project: working paper 3*. Online, available at: www.assessment-reform-group.org (accessed 10 July 2007).

—— (2006c) *Report of Professional Groups Conference*, Online, available at: www.assessment-reform-group.org (accessed 10 July 2007).

Black, P. and Wiliam, D. (1998) 'Assessment and classroom learning', *Assessment in Education*, 5: 7–71.

—— (2006) 'The reliability of assessments', in J. Gardner (ed.) *Assessment and Learning*, London: Sage.

Black, P., Harrison, C., Lee, C., Marshall, B. and Wiliam, D. (2003) *Assessment for Learning: putting it into practice*, Maidenhead: Open University Press.

Crooks, T. (1988) 'The impact of classroom evaluation practices on students', *Review of Educational Research*, 58: 438–81.

Dweck, C.S. (1999) *Self-Theories: their role in motivation, personality and development*, Philadelphia, PA: Psychology Press.

Harlen, W. (2005) 'Trusting teachers' judgments: research evidence of the reliability and validity of teachers' assessment for summative purposes', *Research Papers in Education*, 20: 245–70.

Harlen, W. and Deakin Crick, R. (2003) 'Testing and motivation for learning', *Assessment in Education*, 10: 169–208.

Harlen, W. and James, M. (1997) 'Assessment and learning: differences and relationships between formative and summative assessment', *Assessment in Education*, 4: 365–80.

Johnston, J. and McClune, W. (2000) 'Selection project sel 5.1: pupil motivation and attitudes – self-esteem, locus of control, learning disposition and the impact of selection on teaching and learning', in *The Effects of the Selective System on Secondary Education in Northern Ireland*, Research papers Volume II, Bangor, Co. Down: Department of Education.

Pollard, A., Triggs, P., Broadfoot, P., McNess, E. and Osborn, M. (2000) *What Pupils Say: changing policy and practice in primary education*, London: Continuum.

PWC (2004) *Financial Modelling of the English Exams System 2003–4*, report from PriceWaterhouseCoopers (PWC) for the QCA (2004).

SCRE (1995) *Taking a Closer Look at Science*, Edinburgh: Scottish Council for Research in Education.

Technology in the service of twenty-first century learning and assessment

Martin Ripley

technology can add value to assessment practice in a variety of ways ... e-assessment in fact is much more than just an alternative way of doing what we already do.

(JISC, 2006b: 7)

Introduction

Consider the following two accounts:

> In 2006 one of the UK's largest awarding bodies, the Assessment and Quali-fications Alliance (AQA), completed its first trial of computer-delivered assessment at GCSE. The approach taken by AQA was to create a closed-response computer-delivered test as one component of a science GCSE. The on-screen test was created by selecting suitable materials from past paper-based tests. The AQA pilot was critically reviewed by the national media, who were sceptical of the value of multiple-choice testing. Jonathan Osborne, Professor of Science Education at King's College London said: 'How is this going to assess pupils' ability to express themselves in scientific language, a major aspect of science?' The Times article expressed strong doubt regarding the educational value of this approach to testing, a view shared by many educators in the UK.
>
> (*Times Online*, 2006)

Over the past decade, there has been unprecedented enthusiasm for the potential of technology to transform learning. The Department for Education and Skills (DfES) has provided significant sums of money for schools to purchase computer equipment and networks, to buy content and manage-ment systems. There have been nationwide training and development programmes for teachers and headteachers. And yet, by 2007, most informed commentators have estimated that fewer than 15% of schools in England have embedded technology in their teaching and learning. Ofsted reported that none of the schools in their 2005–06 inspections had embedded ICT.

(Ofsted, 2006: 78)

The first report reflects a widely held perception that technology 'dumbs down' education and learning. In this view, e-assessment is often perceived to involve multiple choice testing. The second report reflects a vision of learning in the twenty-first century (albeit as yet unrealized) that uses technology to personalize learning, with learners increasingly in control of their own learning. In this view, e-assessment is seen as a catalyst for change, bringing transformation of learning, pedagogy and curricula.

Assessment embodies what is valued in education. Assessment – whether in the form of examinations, qualifications, tests, homework, grading policies, reports to parents or what the teacher praises in the classroom – sets the educational outcomes.

To meet the educational challenges of the twenty-first century assessment must embody the twenty-first century learning skills such as self-confidence, communication, working together and problem solving. In addition, assessment must support learners' analysis of their own learning and it must support constructivist approaches to learning.

Defining e-assessment

For the purposes of this chapter, a broad definition of e-assessment is needed (based on JISC, 2006a: 43):

- e-assessment refers to the use of technology to digitize, make more efficient, redesign or transform assessment
- assessment includes the requirements of examinations, qualifications, national curriculum tests, school based testing, classroom assessment and assessment for learning
- the focus of e-assessment might be any of the participants within assessment processes – the learners, teachers, school managers, assessment providers, examiners, awarding bodies.

Overview

This chapter discusses the ways in which schools can use technology and assessment to support and transform learning in the twenty-first century. It is divided into five parts:

1. The policy framework for e-assessment, which summarizes the major policies that relate to e-assessment.

2. Aspects of e-assessment, which provides a description of what counts as e-assessment.

3. The benefits for learners and learning, which outlines the major reasons why a school might wish to consider e-assessment.

4. Embedding e-assessment in teaching and learning, which reviews the use of e-assessment in schools and surveys major products available in the marketplace.

5. Research evidence underpinning e-assessment developments, which summarizes major research evidence for the efficacy of e-assessment.

The policy framework for e-assessment

In 2005 Ken Boston, the Chief Executive of the Qualifications and Curriculum Authority (QCA) spoke optimistically of a forthcoming transformation of assessment in which technology was presented as a catalyst for change: 'technology for assessment and reporting is the third of three potentially transformative but still incomplete major reforms' (Boston, 2005).

His speech continued by setting out the agenda in order that technology-enabled assessment might fulfil its potential. He described the following three challenges:

- reforming assessment (i.e. placing more emphasis on assessment for learning, in the classroom, and less emphasis on external examinations)
- improving the robustness of organizations that supply assessments (i.e. ensuring that awarding bodies make the change)
- leading debate regarding standards and comparability with paper-based ancestors of e-assessments (i.e. making sure that transformation is not thwarted by media hype about erosion of standards and 'dumbing down').

Whilst acknowledging the risks and difficult choices for suppliers and adopters of e-assessment, Ken Boston's speech concluded with an enthusiastic call for technology to be used to transform assessment and learning:

> There is much less risk, and immensely greater gain, in pursuing strategies based on transformational onscreen testing; transformational question items and tasks; total learning portfolio management; process-based marking; and life-long learner access to systemic and personal data. There is no political downside in evaluating skills and knowledge not possible with existing pencil and paper tests, nor in establishing a new time series of performance targets against which to report them.
>
> (Boston, 2005)

Surprisingly, much of QCA's subsequent policy developments and e-assessment activity has failed to provide the transformation that Ken Boston spoke of. Activity has been regulatory and reactive, not visionary and not providing the necessary leadership. For example, QCA has published two regulatory reviews of issues relating to the use of technology in assessment. The first study focused on issues relating to e-plagiarism (QCA, 2005) and led QCA to establish an advisory team in this area. Some commentators have seen a link between the e-plagiarism study and the subsequent advice from QCA that will lead to significant curtailments in the use of coursework. QCA's second review related to the use of technology to cheat in examination halls (QCA, 2006).

There is a dilemma here for the regulators. At the same time as wanting to demonstrate regulatory control and enhance public confidence in examination systems, the regulatory bodies have wanted to bring about transformation. So, while QCA has been urged to consider banning digital devices, projects (like eSCAPE – see below) have been demonstrating the improvements to assessment that those very same devices can bring.

At the present time, some of the government's flagship education reforms include significant opportunity for assessment reform generally and for e-assessment in particular. Four core elements of government policy are directed to achieving change:

- the Every Child Matters reforms
- curriculum remodelling, including QCA's review of the key stage 3 curriculum, the government's 14–19 reforms, and the introduction of specialized diplomas
- the 'personalisation' of the curriculum
- the Building Schools for the Future (BSF) programme.

There is significant potential within these reforms for technology-led transformation of assessment. First, the 14–19 reforms are designed in part to provide learners with greater flexibility and control over their learning and assessment. As learning becomes increasingly fluid over time and place, so assessment systems will have to provide learners with greater flexibility. Local authorities, required to provide a 'local prospectus' setting out the range of learning opportunities for 14–19-year-olds, will provide e-portfolio systems to support learners.

Second, the DfES's 14–19 reform programme has also carried forward Sir Mike Tomlinson's recommendation that a new assessment, in the form of an extended essay/project, should be introduced. The currently agreed assessment framework states that 'the evidence for assessment for any part of the project, including its outcome, can be presented in any appropriate format, for example written text, notes, slides, CD-ROMs, videos/DVDs of performances and activities, audio tape, photographs and artefacts'.

Third, QCA is currently field testing the new national Qualifications and Credit Framework to enable learners to build up a record of achievements and credit over time and with different awarding bodies. Qualifications will be broken down into a national framework of units, learners will record credit by unit and will be able to accumulate the credit needed for a qualification. A national IT solution will be required for learners to access their record of qualifications and to 'cash-in' their unit credits with designated awarding bodies.

Finally, the Gilbert 2020 Vision report addressed the role that technology has to play in delivering personalised learning. The report made clear that technology affects what, how and why a student learns. It also drew attention to the role of technology in providing timely access to assessment information for the learner:

> While all schools have systems for recording and reporting information about pupils and their achievement, this information is not always readily available to those who could draw on it to improve learning, namely the classroom teachers, pupils and parents. Using the new technologies to inform learning and teaching will be a priority.
>
> (DfES, 2006: 26)

Points for reflection

1. Review the new regulatory guidance published by QCA and its sister regulatory bodies (QCA, 2007a).
2. Review Christine Gilbert's 2020 Vision report (DfES, 2006) especially the views it offers on the role of technology in developing twenty-first century learning.

Aspects of e-assessment

To understand the contribution of technology through e-assessment we must understand the ways in which it redefines the relationship among learning, the curriculum, pedagogy and assessment. At its most straightforward, e-assessment replicates paper-based approaches to testing. For example, there are several commercially available products that supply national curriculum test materials on-screen and on CD-ROM, most of which consist of libraries of past test papers. At the other end of the spectrum, however, e-assessment changes pedagogy and assists students in taking responsibility for their learning. It extends significantly our concept of what counts as learning in the classroom, and it supports out-of-school learning.

Table 10.1 sets out the range of ways in which different types of e-assessment product support different aspects of learning. In the most sophisticated examples

Table 10.1 e-assessment products to support learning

Type of product	Examples	Classroom benefits	Issues
Digital learning space	*Digital brain* *UniServity Connected Learning Community (CLC)*	Learner driven Constructivist Encourages learners to review progress in learning	Few applications Most become diverted into mechanical e-portfolios and content rich learning platforms
21st century higher order skills	*KS3 ICT tests* *World Class Tests* *Maths Grid Club?*	Drives 21st century curriculum; higher order skills; communication and problem solving; focus on applying skills and knowledge	Very few resources; often focused on mathematics; require schools to welcome the curriculum changes that this brings
Classroom-based handheld technology	*Wolverhampton's* *Learn2Go pilot* *Prometheon Activpad*	Every pupil has constant access to the technology, enabling true embedding; supports the characteristics of assessment for learning	Emerging technology, not yet established; requires significant energy and commitment from a school to make this work
E-portfolios and related assessment activities	*Measuring Pupil Performance (MPP)* *MAPS, from TAG Learning*	Pupil can 'drive' the assessment; assessment criteria are visible	
Drill and review	*Jelly James*	Can focus on misconceptions and weakness	
Databases of past test papers	*Testbase* *Exampro* *Trumptech* *TestWise*	Provides the teacher with highest quality assessment items, that can be flexibility arranged to create focused tests	Often restricted to test format, but can still offer good diagnostic capability
Analysis tools	*Pupil Tracker*	Aids preparation for tests and examinations, supports the focus on school performance tables	Can be mechanical and results focused, not learning focused

Scale of increasing technological sophistication and learning redesign of digital learning, assessment is blended so well with learning that the two become indistinguishable.

E-portfolios are one of the e-assessment tools that feature strongly in government policy thinking. *Harnessing Technology* (DfES, 2005: 18) expresses an aim for 'online personalized support for learners, parents, and practitioners, giving secure access to personal records, online resources, tracking and assessment that works across all sectors, communities, and relevant public and private organizations'.

It is not just the DfES that sees e-portfolios as a key tool for linking assessment and learning. At a system level, several bodies have begun to look to e-portfolio systems, integrated with learning, to transform the student's experience. One agency, the National Academy for Gifted and Talented Youth (NAGTY) at the University of Warwick, has developed criteria for e-portfolio systems:

- help improve provision in schools ... by providing a sharper focus on needs of individuals
- enable recording of full range of learning including formal achievements such as exams but also informal learning especially in wider schooling (enrichment)
- enable progression planning, guidance, creation and tracking of personal pathways
- help individuals to take control of their learning
- present records for a variety of audiences
- ensure that pupils learn more about their own personal strengths and weaknesses so as to build on strengths and mitigate weaknesses
- ensure that opportunities offered match educational needs, both in and out of school
- ensure pupils are able to present themselves optimally at points of transfer, especially school to HEI.

This list of descriptors reflects a view that e-portfolios should support learning. Their contributions include the recognition of learning in a wide range of contexts, systems that support and guide learners, monitoring progress, and supporting students to reflect on learning and become increasingly self-aware. All of these are characteristics of assessment for learning.

An e-portfolio is not a technological toy designed to do new things, with the key issue for schools being which e-portfolio product to buy. Instead the question is a much broader one about the strategic use of technology to help schools meet their wider educational aims.

An example of strategic development at local authority level can be found in the Wolverhampton system, which has three components. Virtual Workspace is an 'open all hours' learning resource for 16–19-year-olds. It provides students with mentors and tutors, able to respond to requests for help by email or telephone. Students have access to online course material, and technical training and support are available for school staff. For the second component, 'Area prospectus', all 14–16 providers in the area have agreed to enable learners to take courses across a range of institutions. To make this possible they use common names for courses and have designated one day of the week when learners can physically move to other institutions to attend lessons. The third component is a piece of software called 'My i-plan', which records what students are planning to do and how they are progressing. Importantly, it operates through a system of dual logins, providing students with a degree of control and ownership.

Wolverhampton's work is preparing the local authority for the effects of national policy changes that will transform the face of secondary schooling. Those policy changes will provide learners with more flexibility in where and when they learn, and will require modern assessment systems able to follow the learner and accredit a wide range of evidence of learning. E-portfolios and e-assessment have a fundamental role to play in joining learning with assessment and enabling the learner to monitor progress.

Points for reflection

1. Review the strategic design of Wolverhampton's 14–19 provision, and the enabling role of technology.
2. Consider whether your school has, or is part of, a wider plan for the strategic use of technology to support educational transformation.

The benefits of e-assessment

There are a number of compelling reasons why school leaders should consider e-assessment.

1. *It has a positive effect on motivation and performance.* Strong claims are made for the positive effect of technology on pupils' attitudes to learning. E-books have been found to increase boys' willingness to read and improve the quality of their writing (Perry, 2005). Anecdotal evidence suggests that the concentration and performance of even our youngest learners improve when they are using technology. Adult learners self-labelled as school and exam failures have said that e-assessment removes the stress and anxiety they associate with traditional approaches to examinations.

    The Learn2Go project in Wolverhampton has experimented with the use of handheld devices in primary and secondary schools (Whyley, 2007). Already this project has demonstrated significant improvements in children's self-assessment, motivation and engagement with the curriculum, including in reading and mathematics. The work is now also claiming evidence that these broad gains translate into improvements in children's scores on more traditional tests.

2. *It frees up teacher time.* Well managed, e-assessment approaches can certainly free up significant amounts of teacher time. Some e-assessment products provide teachers with quality test items and teachers can store and share assessments they create. Where appropriate, auto-marking can enable a teacher to focus on analysis and interpretation of assessment results.

3. *High quality assessment resources.* High quality, valid and reliable assessments are notoriously difficult to design. E-assessment resources provide every teacher with access to high quality materials – whether as a CD-ROM containing past questions from national examinations, or as a database of classroom projects with marking material for standardization purposes, or as websites with interactive problem-solving activities.

4. *Provides rich diagnostic information.* E-assessment applications are beginning to provide learners and teachers with detailed reports that describe strengths and weaknesses. For example some examinations provide the student not only with an instant result but also with a report setting out any specific areas for further study; some early reading assessments provide the teacher with weekly reports and highlight children whose progress might be at risk.

There is a distinction to be drawn between the genuinely diagnostic and learner focused reports that some software provides, versus the 'progress tracking' reports available through other products. The purpose of progress tracking reports is to ensure that pupils achieve targeted national curriculum and GCSE results, and they are quite different from diagnostic reporting.

5. *Flexible and easy to use.* One of the strongest arguments in favour of e-assessment is that it makes the timing of assessment flexible. Formal assessments can be conducted when the learner is ready, without having to wait for the annual set day. Many providers of high-stakes assessments nowadays require no more than 24 hours' notice of a learner wanting to sit an examination. Diagnostic assessments can be provided quickly, and at the relevant time.

6. *Links learning and assessment, empowering the learner.* One of the core principles of assessment for learning is that assessment should inform learning. The learner is therefore the prime intended audience for assessment information. E-assessment tools can provide ways of achieving this – for example, e-portfolios should always enable the learner to collect assessment information, reflect on that information and make decisions (with the support of a teacher when appropriate) about future learning steps.

7. *Assessment of high order thinking skills in ways not possible with paper and pencil testing.* World Class Tests, developed by QCA, are designed to assess higher order thinking skills in mathematics and problem solving for students aged 9–14. They are one of the best examples of computer-enabled assessments and have set expectations for the design of on-screen assessment.

8. *It is inevitable.* An increasing range of assessments is being developed for use on computer. Few of us can apply for a job without being required to complete an on-screen assessment; many professional examinations are now administered on-screen; whole categories of qualification (such as key skills tests) are now predominantly administered on-screen. Awarding bodies are already introducing e-assessments into GCSEs and A-levels. The QCA has set a 'Vision and blueprint', launched in 2004 by the then Secretary of State for Education and Skills, Charles Clarke, which heralds significant use of e-assessment by 2009 (QCA, 2004). The question is not so much whether a school should plan for e-assessment, but why a school would wish to wait and delay.

These descriptions of the benefits to teachers and learners of e-assessment are compelling. It is also clear that the primary benefit of e-assessment is that it supports effective classroom learning in accordance with the characteristics of assessment for learning.

Points for reflection

1. Document the intended learning benefits of e-assessment, and evaluate the extent to which your implementation delivers those benefits.

2. Use case studies and other resources available from the following bodies (accessed 10 July 2007) to build knowledge and inform your e-assessment choices:
   - www.futurelab.org.uk
   - www.e-assessmentassociation.com
   - www.21stcenturylearningalliance.com
   - www.qca.org.uk
   - www.jisc.ac.uk.

3. Can schools in the twenty-first century ignore e-assessment?

Embedding e-assessment in teaching and learning

This part of the chapter provides a review of two contrasting, but equally successful, classroom approaches to using e-assessment technology to transform students' learning experience in line with the principles of assessment for learning.

Example one: using handheld technology in the classroom

One of the most interesting recent developments is the increasing availability of small, interactive handheld devices, which are technologically robust and relatively cost effective. At their simplest these devices enable pupils to select a response option to a question or issue, resembling multiple choice activities. However, the technology is potentially much more educationally powerful than this suggests, and can be used to support effective questioning (see the chapter by Jeremy Hodgen and Mary Webb in this volume). By enabling every pupil to respond simultaneously, and analysing their responses, the technology can play a vital role in supporting assessment for learning.

In one school mathematics teachers experimented with the use of handheld technology, setting mathematical problems for the students to solve. Each pupil had their own device, but the activity required the students to work together and exchange ideas. The evaluators of this study were unequivocal in citing the learning benefits.

> One of the classroom teachers summarized the situation by saying, 'Why did they succeed? Because they were thinking, not spouting memorized facts. Because there was no pressure … no boring worksheets asking kids to do the same thing over and over. Because there were no wrong answers; that is, a child could say anything sensible and the others would react to it and comment on it and the child would grow stronger in his or her conclusion or alter it in response to what other kids said. Because they were thinking and the judgment of their thinking was whether it made sense to them and to others rather than a teacher's judgment and red marks on a test paper.'
>
> (O'Brien, 2006)

Similarly, at Strathclyde University the Department of Mechanical Engineering has about 580 students. The department's lecturers complained about a number of related problems: students were having difficulty in understanding core concepts; attendance was low; and too many students were dropping out of the courses.

In order to address this problem an electronic voting system, Interwrite™ PRS (Personal Response System), was installed. Students still worked in lecture halls, but were grouped into small groups to work through problems together. Typically a lecture was broken down into short spells of input from the lecturer, followed by the lecturer setting a problem that the students worked on collaboratively. Using the technology, all students could send their responses back to the lecturer and could view the collated responses displayed for the class. The lecturer could immediately see whether students had a good understanding of the concept being taught and could pace the lecture accordingly. The evaluation claimed that:

> ... this increased interactivity has improved understanding and retention. Results from diagnostic tests provide further evidence of raised standards in the department. Allowing time for debate and reflection has prompted more active learning – students feel motivated to focus on knowledge gained during a lecture so that they can perform well in what they see as 'fun' assessment activities. [...] multiple choice questions and peer-to-peer discussion can bring to life the less accessible aspects of a curriculum.
>
> (JISC, 2005: 28)

Handheld technologies provide a useful tool for teachers to develop and strengthen classroom questioning, particularly since every student responds to every question. Individuals or groups can neither dominate classroom discussion nor 'hide' from the teacher by not responding and not exposing misconceptions or gaps in knowledge. Comprehensive assessment information is available for immediate use in the classroom and for later analysis.

Example two: transformative assessment

The eSCAPE project led by Richard Kimbell at the Technology Education Research Unit (TERU) at Goldsmiths College, and by TAG Learning, has focused on GCSE design and technology. Its purpose has been to design short classroom-administered assessments of students' ability to create, prototype, evaluate and communicate a solution to a design challenge. In the eSCAPE project:

- students work individually, but within a group context, to build their design solution
- each student has a PDA, with functionality enabling them to video, photograph, write documents, sketch ideas and record voice messages
- at specified points in the assessment, students exchange ideas and respond to the ideas of others in the group
- at the end of the assessment, students' portfolios are loaded to a secure website, through which human markers score the work.

A report of phase 2 (TERU, 2006) described the 2006 pilot in which over 250 students completed multimedia e-portfolios and submitted these to TERU, who had trained a team of markers to mark the e-portfolios on-screen. The assessment efficacy and the robustness of the technology have proven highly satisfactory. Students work well with the technology and rate the validity of the assessment process positively.

The eSCAPE assessment uses an approach to marking known as Thurstone's graded pairs. Human markers rank order students' work, working through a series of paired portfolios. For each pairing, the markers record which of the two pieces of work is better. Based on the positive evaluation findings of this approach, QCA has encouraged further development and Edexcel is planning to apply the eSCAPE approach.

Commercial databases of tests and examinations

Probably the most commonly used e-assessment resource available to schools is databases of examination and test questions provided by commercial companies.

Points for reflection

1. If you are considering purchasing a major e-assessment tool:
    - What would be your school's aims in using such technology? How do you want it to support learning?
    - How will you support the technology in your school? Who will be responsible for making sure it works?
    - Visit the companies at annual education and technology shows such as the Education show, SETT or BETT.
    - Visit websites – School Zone, e-assessment association, e-assessment question conference.
    - Ask for demo or trial versions.
    - Try them out with children. Ask the children's views.
2. If you are considering purchasing databases of tests or examinations:
    - Who wrote the questions in the database? Are they of high quality?
    - Can they be administered on-screen or do they have to be printed?
    - How often is the question bank replenished? What is the annual cost of an update?
    - How many pupils can use the software?
    - Can pupils access the materials from home?
    - Are the questions in the database linked to the national curriculum and the national strategies?
    - Will you want to create your own question bank? Is this possible?
    - How can responses and results for individual pupils be stored and analysed? How can pupils' results be matched into school IT management information systems? Who will analyse strengths and weaknesses?
    - How will you prevent pupils being set tests too frequently?

Teachers find it useful to have access to databases of past examination and test questions, containing facsimile copies of previous questions and (depending on the product) the flexibility to select specified questions, print onto paper, assign electronically, edit or add questions. Different types of products are described and evaluated in Table 10.2.

Developments and research

There have been few studies of technology's impact on learning of technology. Some studies have found that frequent use of technology in school and at home correlates with improved examination performance on the traditional, paper-based tests used at key stage 3 and GCSE (Harrison *et al.*, 2002). However, it is not clear whether it is technology that makes the difference, or whether technology tends to exist in families and social groups more likely to do well in traditional measures of educational performance. This research should be compared with the Education Testing Service study referred to below, which found different effects for some students taking tests on computer.

Developments and research in e-assessment are in their early days, but a growing body of evidence is accumulating, some of which is reviewed below.

Scotland

The e-assessment work of the Scottish Qualifications Authority (SQA) includes Pass-IT (which investigated how e-assessments might enhance flexibility, improve attainment and support teaching and learning) and guidelines on e-assessment for schools (Pass-IT, 2005). E-assessment has been used in high stakes external examinations including Higher Mathematics and Biotechnology Intermediate 2. The Scottish OnLine Assessment Resources project is developing summative online assessments for a range of units within Higher National qualifications. SQA is developing three linked on-screen assessment tools for Communication, Numeracy and IT, and is also investigating the use of wikis and blogs for assessment (McAlpine, 2006). The SCHOLAR programme developed within Heriot-Watt University provides students with an online virtual college designed to help students as they progress between school, college and university.

Key stage 3 ICT tests

The key stage 3 ICT test project is one of the largest and most expensive e-assessment developments in the world. The original vision for the tests involved the creation of an entire virtual world, with students responding to sophisticated

Table 10.2 Test and examination resources

	Databases of 'past papers', covering key stage 2 and 3, GCSE and A levels	Software containing bespoke test content	Software that enables teachers to generate test questions or assessment items.
What are they?	Products consist of past key stage 2 and 3 test papers, with past optional test questions available too. Other products, aligned to specific awarding bodies, focus on providing past GCSE and A-level papers. There are one or two key stage 1 products.	A number of assessment providers and educational publishers now supply a range of test material on computer. These cover national curriculum subjects.	These are sometime referred to as 'question authoring tools'. They provide teachers with the structure for a number of basic question types, enabling the teacher to author their own questions. The key advantage of this approach is that student answers are easily captured and marked electronically. In some cases the software enables the teacher to administer the test on-computer.
Design for classroom use?	Most of these systems provide 'teacher-only' versions. This means the teacher needs to print and distribute hard copy tests. A key issue to consider here is marking – the more automated the marking, the more narrowly focused the questions tend to be.	Provide everyday access to an increasing range of tests, including cognitive ability tests, national curriculum tests (some suppliers cover most subjects for most key stages), batteries of mental arithmetic tests and spelling rules, reading record assessments, key and basic skills tests.	Teachers can create, save and share assessment items. Importantly, these should be thought of as enabling the teacher to create open-ended questions (to facilitate thinking, collaboration and communication) as well as including closed response questions (which have a clear, correct response).
What are the key strengths in supporting AfL?	Can be used to focus exam revision, for example, by helping the learner identify gaps in knowledge. Teachers can create bespoke assessments, covering specified levels or areas of the programme of study. Provide teachers with test questions of the highest quality.	Support assessment when ready. Cover a widening range of curriculum subjects and skill areas. Can be used on an individual basis. Provide teachers with good quality assessments. Provide good tools to identify specific strengths and weaknesses.	Teachers can design and tailor questions to meet specific classroom needs. Assessment can be conducted with individual students, groups or as whole class activities. They can enable teachers to probe misunderstandings, to encourage collaborative thinking and to cover all areas of the taught curriculum, not just those elements that feature in statutory tests or in qualifications.
What are the key assessment weaknesses?	Can be overused for test drill. Focus only on exam/test content; other areas of learning are not covered.	Can be overused in test mode (i.e. students are required to work in test conditions). There is no external verification of validity and reliability of test content.	The test questions will not have national performance information associated with them so teachers will not know how accurate their students' performance compares to a national picture of strengths and weaknesses.

problems within the virtual world. For this vision to work, the project needed to deliver successful innovation on several fronts, for example:

- developing the virtual world
- developing a successful test form within the virtual world, including a test that could reliably measure students' use of their ICT skills
- developing a new psychometric model
- training all secondary schools in the technical and educational adoption of the tests
- redesigning the teaching of ICT.

However, the full range of planned innovation has not been delivered. In particular, the tests have adopted more traditional approaches to test design, and teachers generally have not been persuaded that the tests reflect improved practice in ICT teaching. Nevertheless, the project is one of the most evaluated e-assessment projects (see for example QCA, 2007b) and is an excellent source of information for other organizations considering the development of innovative forms of e-assessment.

Twenty-first century skills assessments

Margaret Honey led a worldwide investigation into the existence and quality of assessments in key areas of twenty-first century learning (Partnership for 21st Century Skills, 2006). Her report highlighted 'promising assessments' including England's key stage 3 ICT tests. She found that although educators in many countries agree that ICT skills are core learning skills, it is only in the UK that substantial progress has been made in developing school-based assessment of ICT. Honey was unable to find any measures that address students' understanding of global and international issues, although she reported that in the USA assessment of civic engagement is quite well established. Also in the USA, an assessment of financial, economic and business literacy is currently being developed and will become mandatory for students in year 12.

Technical measurement issues

In 2005 the Education Testing Service (ETS) published the findings of a large scale comparison of paper-based and computer-delivered assessments (National Centre for Education Statistics, 2005). The empirical data were collected in 2001 and involved over 2,500 year 8 students who completed either mathematics or writing assessments. The traditional, paper-based tests were migrated to screen format, with little or no amendment made for the purpose of screen delivery. In mathematics the study found no significant differences between performance on paper and on screen, except for those students reporting at least one parent with a degree. These students performed better on paper. The study also found no significant differences in writing, expect for students from urban fringe/large town locations. Again these students performed better on paper than on screen. The purpose of the ETS study was to investigate the efficacy of migrating existing eight grade tests from paper to screen. The study concluded that this was achievable, although with some loss of unsuitable test items. The study did not examine the issue of whether such a migration would be educationally desirable nor whether computer-delivered tests should include an aim to transform test content.

Market surveys

Thompson Prometric commissioned two reviews of e-assessment issues involving all UK awarding bodies (Thompson Prometric, 2005, 2006). They achieved high levels of participation and revealed that the majority of awarding bodies are actively pursuing e-assessment, although often without senior executive or strategic involvement. The studies made clear the remarkable agreement between awarding bodies regarding the benefits of e-assessment, which included learner choice, flexibility and on-demand assessment. There was also agreement between most awarding bodies regarding the major issues – authentication, security, cost and technical reliability.

Conclusions

In the words of Ken Boston, there is much to be gained by considering the transformative potential of e-assessment. This chapter has sought to describe the importance of linking e-assessment to strategic planning for the future of learning, as well as identifying a number of ways in which e-assessment can support effective learning in the classroom.

In a significant recent development, an eAssessment Association (eAA) has been created by Cliff Beevers, Emeritus Professor of Mathematics at Heriot-Watt University. The group was launched in March 2007, with involvement from industry, users and practitioners. The eAA aims to provide members with professional support, provide a vision and national leadership of e-assessment, and publish a statement of good practice for commercial vendors. It is to be hoped that the eAA will play a significant role in encouraging the assessment community to make use of technology to improve assessment for learners.

Further reading

e-Assessment Association. Online, available at: www.e-assessmentassociation.com (accessed 10 July 2007).

MacFarlane, A. (2005) *Assessment for the Digital Age*. Online, available at: www.qca.org.uk/libraryAssets/media/11479_mcfarlane_assessment_for_the_digital_age.pdf (accessed 10 July 2007).

Microsoft (2005) *Wolverhampton City Council mobilises learning to give students access to anywhere, anytime education*. Online, available at: download.microsoft.com/documents/customerevidence/8097_Wolverhampton_Final.doc (accessed 10 July 2007).

Naismith, L., Lonsdale, P., Vavoula, G. and Sharples, M. (2004) *Literature Review in Mobile Technologies and Learning*, Futurelab Report Series no. 11.

Pass-IT (2007) 'Pass-IT – Project on Assessment in Scotland using Information Technology'. Online, available at: www.pass-it.org.uk (accessed 10 July 2007).

Ridgway, J. (2004) *e-Assessment Literature Review*. Online, available at: www.futurelab.org.uk/resources/publications_reports_articles/literature_reviews/Literature_Review204 (accessed 10 July 2007).

Ripley, M. (2007) Futurelab e-Assessment Literature Review – an update. Online, available at: www.futurelab.org.uk (accessed 13 November 2007).

Scholar Programme. Online, available at: scholar.hw.ac.uk (accessed 10 July 2007).

Scottish Qualifications Authority (2005) *SQA Guidelines on e-Assessment for Schools*, SQA Dalkeith, Publication code: BD2625, June. Online, available at: www.sqa.org.uk/files_ccc/SQA_Guidelines_on_e-assessment_Schools_June05.pdf (accessed 10 July 2007).

References

Boston, K. (2005) 'Strategy, technology and assessment', speech delivered to the Tenth Annual Round Table Conference, Melbourne, October. Online, available at: www.qca.org.uk/qca_8581.aspx (accessed 10 July 2007).

DfES (2005) *Harnessing Technology*. Online, available at: www.dfes.gov.uk/publications/e-strategy/ (accessed 10 July 2007).

—— (2006) *2020 Vision: report of the teaching and learning in 2020 review group*, London: DfES. Online, available at: www.teachernet.gov.uk/educationoverview/briefing/strategyarchive/whitepaper2005/teachingandlearning 2020/ (accessed 10 July 2007).

Harrison, C., Comber, C., Fisher, T., Haw, K., Lewin, C., Lunzer, E., McFarlane, A., Mavers, D., Scrimshaw, P., Somekh, B. and Watling, R. (2002) *ImpaCT2: the impact of information and communication technologies on pupil learning and attainment*. Online, available at: www.becta.org.uk/research/impact2 (accessed 10 July 2007).

JISC (2005) *Innovative Practice with e-Learning: a good practice guide to embedding mobile and wireless technologies into everyday practice*. Online, available at: www.jisc.ac.uk/uploaded_documents/InnovativePE.pdf (accessed 10 July 2007).

—— (2006a) *e-Assessment Glossary – extended*. Online, available at: www.jisc.ac.uk/uploaded_documents/-eAssess-Glossary-Extended-v1-01.pdf (accessed 10 July 2007).

—— (2006b) *Effective Practice with e-Assessment: an overview of technologies, policies and practice in further and higher education*. Online, available at: www.jisc.ac.uk/media/documents/themes/elearning/effprac_eassess.pdf (accessed 10 July 2007).

McAlpine, M. (2006) Using Wikis to Access Collaborative Achievement. Online, available at: future/ab.org.uk/resources/publications_reports_articles/web_articles/Web_Article464 (accessed 10 July 2007).

National Centre for Education Statistics (2005) *Online Assessment in Mathematics and Writing. Reports from the NAEP technology-based assessment project, research and development series*. Online, available at: nces.ed.gov/pubsearch/pubsinfo.asp?pubid=2005457 (accessed 10 July 2007).

O'Brien, T.C. (2006) *Observing Children's Mathematical Problem Solving with 21st Century Technology*. Online, available at: www.handheldlearning.co.uk/content/view/24/2/ (accessed 10 July 2007).

Ofsted (2006) *The Annual Report of Her Majesty's Chief Inspector of schools, 2005–06*. Online, available at: www.ofsted.gov.uk/assets/Internet_Content/Shared_Content/Files/annualreport0506.pdf (accessed 10 July 2007).

Partnership for 21st Century Skills (2006) *The Assessment Landscape*. Online, available at: www.21stcenturyskills.org/images/stories/otherdocs/Assessment_Landscape.pdf (accessed 10 July 2007).

Pass-IT (2005) *Developing ICT-based Assessments for Formative and Summative Purposes*. Online, available at: pass-it.org.uk/project_materials.asp (accessed 10 July 2007).

Perry, D. (2005) *Wolverhampton LEA 'Learn2Go' Mobile Learning PDAs in Schools Project, evaluation phase 1, end of first year report*. Online, available at: www.learning2go.org/pages/evaluation-and-impact.php (accessed 10 July 2007).

QCA (2004) *QCA's e-Assessment Vision*. Online, available at: www.qca.org.uk/qca_5414.aspx (accessed 10 July 2007).

—— (2005) *A review of GCE and GCSE Coursework Arrangements*. Online, available at: www.qca.org.uk/qca_10097.aspx (accessed 10 July 2007).

—— (2006) *Digital Technologies and Dishonesty in Examinations and Tests*. Online, available at: www.qca.org.uk/qca_10079.aspx (accessed 10 July 2007).

—— (2007a) *Regulatory Principles for e-Assessment*. Online, available at: /www.qca.org.uk/qca_10475.aspx (accessed 10 July 2007).

—— (2007b) *A Review of the Key Stage 3 ICT Test*. Online, available at: www.naa.org.uk/naaks3/361.asp (accessed 10 July 2007).

Thompson Prometric (2005) *Drivers and Barriers to the Adoption of e-Assessment for UK Awarding Bodies*, Thompson Prometric.

—— (2006) *Acceptance and Usage of e-Assessment for UK Awarding Bodies*. Online, available at: www.prometric.com/NR/rdonlyres/eegssex2sh6ws72b7qjmfd22n5neltew3fpxeuwl2kbvwbnkw2ww2jbodaskp-spvvqbhmucch3gnlgo3t7d5xpm57mg/060220PrintReady.pdf (accessed 10 July 2007).

TERU (2006) e-scape portfolio assessment phase 2 report. Online, available at: www.teru.org.uk (accessed 13 November 2007).

Times Online (2006) *Select One from Four for a Science GCSE* by Tony Halpin. Online, available at: www.timesonline.co.uk/article/0,,22219509,00.html (accessed 10 July 2007).

Whyley, D. (2007) *Learning2Go Project*. Online, available at: www.learning2go.org/ (accessed 10 July 2007).

Continuing the exploration

Sue Swaffield

Reading the chapters in this volume will have unlocked and opened up under-standing about many key issues in assessment. The authors have explained the relevance to learning and teaching of the ideas they explore, and have used evid-ence from research and practice to develop their arguments. They have proposed points for reflection, provided sources of further reading and suggested implica-tions for practice. Thus the book serves as a guide to the fascinating and hugely important area of assessment. There are many ways in which the exploration can continue, and many possible directions to take.

Unlocking Assessment addresses issues that are absolutely central to the under-standing of assessment, but it is a subject so wide ranging that there are always other aspects awaiting consideration. In any single book some topics will of necessity have been dealt with in passing or not addressed at all. Examples include differences in the assessment process among subjects, and diagnostic assessment of special educational needs. Equity issues such as the ways boys and girls respond to different kinds of assessment, and assessment (both of and for learning) of pupils with English as an additional language or from different cultural backgrounds remain relatively unexplored in the assessment literature. Examination setting, marking and moderation, the measurement of standards over time, and inter-national comparisons of attainment are complete areas of specialism in their own right. The choice of the particular area of assessment for attention by a teacher or a school should be guided by professional concern and a determination to provide the very best learning opportunities for young people.

Whatever the specific focus for exploration, many routes are possible although some prove more rewarding and fruitful than others. A very powerful and prac-tical way of unlocking our own understanding of assessment is by applying insights to practice in our own context, and reflecting on the effects. Many teachers are engaging in various forms of classroom-based enquiry, a process that is particularly enriching when undertaken with colleagues and in partnership with pupils. Dialogue, the consideration of alternative perspectives and the involve-ment of others including parents, all have important parts to play.

There are many sources of support and an ever-growing knowledge base to assist teachers in such activity. Practitioners, networks of schools, professional organizations, local authorities, government agencies and universities are all providing practical assistance, advice and resources to assist continuing enquiry. A number of significant messages can be identified, including: the importance of taking time and not trying to do everything at once; the value of working with others; starting from present practice and concerns; keeping notes to aid reflection; and maintaining an optimistic, critical stance.

When continuing our exploration of assessment and applying our understanding into practice, it is helpful to have a few key points to guide us. In summary:

- assessment reflects what we value
- assessment should be aligned with our beliefs about learning
- the prime purpose of assessment is to assist learning, helping young people grow as learners
- the quality of assessment determines the quality of the conclusions we draw
- practice should be guided by principles.

The rewards that come from reflecting on assessment and applying our understanding to practice are immense, both for students' learning and professional satisfaction. Every teacher will feel and express this in their own way, but the comments of one may resonate with many. A teacher engaged in enquiring into assessment in her classroom reflected upon her 'increased ability to listen to the children, to understand their thinking, and to adjust what I am teaching to their real needs. One small change in my teaching strategy can lead to big changes in some children's learning'.

Index